Gretchen Bitterlin
Dennis Johnson
Donna Price
Sylvia Ramirez
K. Lynn Savage, Series Editor

Ventures 2

STUDENT'S BOOK

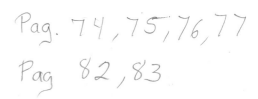
Pag. 74, 75, 76, 77
Pag 82, 83

CAMBRIDGE
UNIVERSITY PRESS

CAMBRIDGE UNIVERSITY PRESS
Cambridge, New York, Melbourne, Madrid, Cape Town,
Singapore, São Paulo, Delhi, Mexico City

Cambridge University Press
32 Avenue of the Americas, New York, NY 10013–2473, USA

www.cambridge.org
Information on this title: www.cambridge.org/9780521548397

First published 2008
13th printing 2013

Printed in Hong Kong, China, by Golden Cup Printing Company Limited

A catalog record for this publication is available from the British Library.

ISBN 978-0-521-54839-7 pack consisting of Student's Book and Audio CD
ISBN 978-0-521-67959-6 Workbook
ISBN 978-0-521-69080-5 pack consisting of Teacher's Edition and Teacher's Toolkit Audio CD / CD-ROM
ISBN 978-0-521-67728-8 CDs (Audio)
ISBN 978-0-521-67729-5 Cassettes
ISBN 978-0-521-67584-0 Add Ventures

Art direction, book design, photo research, and layout services: Adventure House, NYC
Audio production: Richard LePage & Associates

Authors' acknowledgments

The authors would like to acknowledge and thank focus group participants and reviewers for their insightful comments, as well as CUP editorial, marketing, and production staffs, whose thorough research and attention to detail have resulted in a quality product.

The publishers would also like to extend their particular thanks to the following reviewers and consultants for their valuable insights and suggestions:

Francesca Armendaris, North Orange County Community College District, Anaheim, California; **Alex A. Baez**, The Texas Professional Development Group, Austin, Texas; **Kit Bell**, LAUSD Division of Adult and Career Education, Los Angeles, California; **Rose Anne Cleary**, Catholic Migration Office, Diocese of Brooklyn, Brooklyn, New York; **Inga Cristi**, Pima Community College Adult Education, Tucson, Arizona; **Kay De Gennaro**, West Valley Occupational Center, Woodland Hills, California; **Patricia DeHesus**, Illinois Community College Board, Springfield, Illinois; **Magali Apareaida Morais Duignan**, Augusta State University, Augusta, Georgia; **Gayle Fagan**, Harris County Department of Education, Houston, Texas; **Lisa A. Fears**, Inglewood Community Adult School, Inglewood, California; **Jas Gill**, English Language Institute at the University of British Columbia, Vancouver, British Columbia, Canada; **Elisabeth Goodwin**, Pima Community College Adult Education, Tucson, Arizona; **Carolyn Grimaldi**, Center for Immigrant Education and Training, LaGuardia Community College, Long Island City, New York; **Masha Gromyko**, Pima Community College Adult Education, Tucson, Arizona; **Jennifer M. Herrin**, Albuquerque TVI Community College, Albuquerque, New Mexico; **Giang T. Hoang**, Evans Community Adult School, Los Angeles, California; **Karen Hribar**, LAUSD West Valley Occupational Center, Los Angeles, California; **Patricia Ishill**, Union County College, Union County, New Jersey; **Dr. Stephen G. Karel**, McKinley Community School for Adults, Honolulu, Hawaii; **Aaron Kelly**, North Orange County Community College District, Anaheim, California; **Dan Kiernan**, Metro Skills Center, LAUSD, Los Angeles, California; **Kirsten Kilcup**, Green River Community College, Auburn, Washington; **Tom Knutson**, New York Association for New Americans, Inc., New York, New York; **Liz Koenig-Golombek**, LAUSD, Los Angeles, California; **Anita Lemonis**, West Valley Occupational Center, Los Angeles, California; **Lia Lerner**, Burbank Adult School, Burbank, California; **Susan Lundquist**, Pima Community College Adult Education, Tucson, Arizona; **Dr. Amal Mahmoud**, Highline Community College, Des Moines, Washington; **Fatiha Makloufi**, Hostos Community College, Bronx, New York; **Judith Martin-Hall**, Indian River Community College, Fort Pierce, Florida; **Gwen Mayer**, Van Nuys Community Adult School, Los Angeles, California; **Vicki Moore**, El Monte-Rosemead Adult School, El Monte, California; **Jeanne Petrus-Rivera**, Cuyahoga Community College, Cleveland, Ohio; **Pearl W. Pigott**, Houston Community College, Houston, Texas; **Catherine Porter**, Adult Learning Resource Center, Des Plaines, Illinois; **Planaria Price**, Evans Community Adult School, Los Angeles, California; **James P. Regan**, NYC Board of Education, New York, New York; **Catherine M. Rifkin**, Florida Community College at Jacksonville, Jacksonville, Florida; **Amy Schneider**, Pacoima Skills Center, Los Angeles, California; **Bonnie Sherman**, Green River Community College, Auburn, Washington; **Julie Singer**, Garfield Community Adult School, Los Angeles, California; **Yilin Sun**, Seattle Central Community College, Seattle, Washington; **André Sutton**, Belmont Community Adult School, Los Angeles, California; **Deborah Thompson**, El Camino Real Community Adult School, Los Angeles, California; **Evelyn Trottier**, Basic Studies Division, Seattle Central Community College, Seattle, Washington; **Debra Un**, New York University, American Language Institute, New York, New York; **Jodie Morgan Vargas**, Orange County Public Schools, Orlando, Florida; **Christopher Wahl**, Hudson County Community College, Jersey City, New Jersey; **Ethel S. Watson**, Evans Community Adult School, Los Angeles, California; **Barbara Williams**; **Mimi Yang**, Belmont Community Adult School, Los Angeles, California; **Adèle Youmans**, Pima Community College Adult Education, Tucson, Arizona.

Scope and sequence

UNIT TITLE TOPIC	FUNCTIONS	LISTENING AND SPEAKING	VOCABULARY	GRAMMAR FOCUS
Welcome Unit pages 2–5	• Giving personal information – name, address, telephone number, and date of birth • Introducing a classmate • Clarifying spelling • Describing work and life skills	• Asking and answering questions about personal information • Introducing a classmate	• Review of time words	• Review of simple present, present continuous, simple past, and future with *be going to*
Unit 1 **Personal information** pages 6–17 **Topic:** **Describing people**	• Describing height, hair, and eyes • Describing clothing • Describing habitual actions • Describing actions in the present	• Describing what people look like • Asking and describing what people are wearing • Asking and describing what people are doing at the present time • Asking and describing people's habitual actions	• Accessories • Adjectives of size, color, and pattern	• Adjective order • Present continuous vs. simple present
Unit 2 **At school** pages 18–29 **Topic:** **School services**	• Offering advice • Describing wants • Describing future plans	• Asking and describing what people want and need • Asking about and describing future plans	• Computer terms • Vocational courses	• *want* and *need* • Future with *will*
Review: Units 1 and 2 pages 30–31		• Understanding a narrative		
Unit 3 **Friends and family** pages 32–43 **Topic:** **Friends**	• Describing past actions • Describing daily activities • Responding to good and bad news	• Asking and answering questions about past actions • Asking and answering questions about daily habits	• Parts of a car • Daily activities	• Review of simple past with regular and irregular verbs • Simple present vs. simple past
Unit 4 **Health** pages 44–55 **Topic:** **Accidents**	• Identifying appropriate action after an accident • Asking for and giving advice • Expressing necessity • Showing understanding	• Asking for and giving advice • Clarifying meaning	• Health problems • Accidents • Terms on medicine packaging	• *have to* + verb • *should*
Review: Units 3 and 4 pages 56–57		• Understanding a narrative		
Unit 5 **Around town** pages 58–69 **Topic:** **Transportation**	• Identifying methods of transportation • Describing number of times • Describing length of time	• Asking and answering questions about train and bus schedules • Asking and answering questions about personal transportation habits • Describing personal habits	• Train station terms • Travel activities • Adverbs of frequency	• *How often* and *How long* questions • Adverbs of frequency

READING	WRITING	LIFE SKILLS	PRONUNCIATION
• Reading a story about someone's day	• Filling out a library card application	• Reading a library card application • Talking about work skills and life skills	• Pronouncing key vocabulary
• Reading an e-mail about a family member • Scanning to find the answers to questions	• Writing a descriptive paragraph about a classmate • Using a comma after time phrases at the beginning of a sentence	• Reading an order form	• Pronouncing key vocabulary
• Reading a short essay on an application form • Skimming for the main idea	• Writing an expository paragraph about goals • Using *First*, *Second*, and *Third* to organize ideas	• Reading course descriptions • Setting short-term goals	• Pronouncing key vocabulary
			• Recognizing and pronouncing strong syllables
• Reading a personal journal entry • Scanning for *First*, *Next*, and *Finally* to order events	• Writing a personal journal entry about the events of a day • Using a comma after sequence words	• Reading a cell phone calling-plan brochure	• Pronouncing key vocabulary
• Reading a warning label • Understanding a bulleted list	• Filling out an accident report form • Using cursive writing for a signature	• Reading medicine labels	• Pronouncing key vocabulary
			• Recognizing and emphasizing important words
• Reading a personal letter • Scanning for capital letters to determine names of cities and places	• Writing a personal letter about a trip • Spelling out hours and minutes from one to ten in writing	• Reading a bus schedule • Reading a train schedule	• Pronouncing key vocabulary

UNIT TITLE TOPIC	FUNCTIONS	LISTENING AND SPEAKING	VOCABULARY	GRAMMAR FOCUS
Unit 6 Time pages 70–81 **Topic:** Time lines and major events	• Describing major events in the past • Inquiring about life events	• Asking and answering questions about major life events in the past • Ordering events in the past	• Life events	• *When* questions and simple past • Time phrases
Review: Units 5 and 6 pages 82–83		• Understanding a conversation		
Unit 7 Shopping pages 84–95 **Topic:** Comparison shopping	• Comparing price and quality • Comparing two things • Comparing three or more things	• Asking and answering questions to compare furniture, appliances, and stores	• Furniture • Descriptive adjectives	• Comparatives • Superlatives
Unit 8 Work pages 96–107 **Topic:** Work history and job skills	• Identifying job duties • Describing work history	• Asking and answering questions about completed actions • Connecting ideas • Beginning and ending conversations	• Hospital terms • Job duties	• *What* and *Where* questions and simple past • Conjunctions *and, or, but*
Review: Units 7 and 8 pages 108–109		• Understanding a narrative		
Unit 9 Daily living pages 110–121 **Topic:** Solving common problems	• Asking for recommendations • Requesting help politely • Agreeing to a request • Refusing a request politely	• Asking for and making recommendations • Explaining choices • Making polite requests • Agreeing to and refusing requests politely	• Home problems • Descriptive adjectives	• *Which* questions and simple present • Requests with *Can, Could, Will, Would*
Unit 10 Leisure pages 122–133 **Topic:** Special occasions	• Making offers politely • Responding to offers politely	• Making offers politely • Responding to offers politely • Asking and answering questions involving direct and indirect objects	• Celebrations • Party food • Gifts	• *Would you like . . . ?* • Direct and indirect objects
Review: Units 9 and 10 pages 134–135		• Understanding a conversation		

READING	WRITING	LIFE SKILLS	PRONUNCIATION
• Reading a magazine interview • Scanning interview questions to determine what an article is about	• Writing a narrative paragraph about important life events • Using a comma after a time phrase at the beginning of a sentence	• Reading an application for a marriage license • Describing important life events in sequence	• Pronouncing key vocabulary
			• Pronouncing intonation in questions
• Reading a short newspaper article • Guessing the meaning of new words from other words nearby	• Writing a descriptive paragraph about a gift • Using *because* to answer *Why* and to give a reason	• Reading a sales receipt	• Pronouncing key vocabulary
• Reading a letter of recommendation • Scanning text for names and dates	• Writing a summary paragraph about employment history • Capitalizing the names of businesses	• Reading a time sheet	• Pronouncing key vocabulary
			• Pronouncing the *-s* ending in the simple present
• Reading a notice on a notice board • Determining if new words are positive or negative in meaning	• Writing a letter of complaint • Identifying the parts of a letter	• Reading a customer invoice for service and repairs	• Pronouncing key vocabulary
• Reading a narrative paragraph about a party • Looking for examples of the main idea while reading	• Writing a thank-you note for a gift • Indenting paragraphs in an informal note	• Reading a formal invitation to a party	• Pronouncing key vocabulary
			• Pronouncing reduced forms of *Could you* and *Would you*

To the teacher

What is *Ventures*?

Ventures is a five-level, standards-based, integrated-skills series for adult students. The five levels, which are Basic through Level Four, are for low-beginning literacy to high-intermediate students.

The *Ventures* series is flexible enough to be used in open enrollment, managed enrollment, and traditional programs. Its multilevel features support teachers who work with multilevel classes.

What components does *Ventures* have?

Student's Book with Self-study Audio CD

Each **Student's Book** contains a Welcome Unit and ten topic-focused units, plus five review units, one after every two units. Each unit has six skill-focused lessons. Projects, self-assessments, and a reference section are included at the back of the Student's Book.

- **Lessons** are self-contained, allowing for completion within a one-hour class period.

- **Review lessons** recycle, reinforce, and consolidate the materials presented in the previous two units and include a pronunciation activity.

- **Projects** offer community-building opportunities for students to work together, using the Internet or completing a task, such as making a poster or a book.

- **Self-assessments** are an important part of students' learning and success. They give students an opportunity to evaluate and reflect on their learning as well as a tool to support learner persistence.

- The **Self-study Audio CD** is included at the back of the Student's Book. The material on the CD is indicated in the Student's Book by an icon SELF-STUDY AUDIO CD .

Teacher's Edition with Teacher's Toolkit Audio CD/CD-ROM

The interleaved **Teacher's Edition** walks instructors step-by-step through the stages of a lesson.

- Included are learner-persistence and community-building tasks as well as teaching tips, expansion activities, and ways to expand a lesson to two or three instructional hours.

- The Student's Book answer key is included on the interleaved pages in the Teacher's Edition.

- The Teacher's Toolkit Audio CD/CD-ROM contains additional reproducible material for teacher support. Included are picture dictionary cards and worksheets, tests with audio, and student self-assessments for portfolio assessment. Reproducible sheets also include cooperative learning activities. These activities reinforce the materials presented in the Student's Book and develop social skills, including those identified by SCANS[1] as being highly valued by employers.

- The unit, midterm, and final tests are found on both the Teacher's Toolkit Audio CD/CD-ROM and in the Teacher's Edition. The tests include listening, vocabulary, grammar, reading, and writing sections.

Audio Program

The *Ventures* series includes the *Class Audio* and the *Student Self-study Audio* SELF-STUDY AUDIO CD . The Class Audio contains all the listening materials in the Student's Book and is available on CD or audiocassette. The Student Self-study Audio CD contains all the unit conversations, readings, and picture dictionary words from the Student's Book.

Workbook

The **Workbook** has two pages of activities for each lesson in the Student's Book.

- The exercises are designed so learners can complete them in class or independently. Students can check their own answers with the answer key in the back of the Workbook. Workbook exercises can be assigned in class, for homework, or as student support when a class is missed.

- Grammar charts at the back of the Workbook allow students to use the Workbook for self-study.

- If used in class, the Workbook can extend classroom instructional time by 30 minutes per lesson.

Add Ventures

Add Ventures is a book of reproducible worksheets designed for use in multilevel classrooms. The worksheets give students 15–30 minutes additional practice with each lesson and can be used with homogeneous or heterogeneous groupings. These

---

[1] The Secretary's Commission on Achieving Necessary Skills, which produced a document that identifies skills for success in the workplace. For more information, see wdr.doleta.gov/SCANS.

worksheets can also be used as targeted homework practice at the level of individual students, ensuring learner success.

There are three tiered worksheets for each lesson.

- **Tier 1 Worksheets** provide additional practice for those who are at a level slightly below the Student's Book or who require more controlled practice.
- **Tier 2 Worksheets** provide additional practice for those who are on the level of the Student's Book.
- **Tier 3 Worksheets** provide additional practice that gradually expands beyond the text. These multilevel worksheets are all keyed to the same answers for ease of classroom management.

Unit organization

Within each unit there are six lessons:

LESSON A Get ready The opening lesson focuses students on the topic of the unit. The initial exercise, *Talk about the picture*, involves one "big" picture. The visuals create student interest in the topic and activate prior knowledge. They help the teacher assess what learners already know and serve as a prompt for the key vocabulary of each unit. Next is *Listening*, which is based on short conversations. The accompanying exercises give learners the opportunity to relate vocabulary to meaning and to relate the spoken and written forms of new theme-related vocabulary. The lesson concludes with an opportunity for students to practice language related to the theme in a communicative activity, either orally with a partner or individually in a writing activity.

LESSONS B and C focus on grammar. The sections move from a *Grammar focus* that presents the grammar point in chart form; to *Practice* exercises that check comprehension of the grammar point and provide guided practice; and, finally, to *Communicate* exercises that guide learners as they generate original answers and conversations. The sections on these pages are sometimes accompanied by a *Culture note*, which provides information directly related to the conversation practice (such as the use of titles with last names), or a *Useful language* note, which provides several expressions that can be used interchangeably to accomplish a specific language function (such as greetings).

LESSON D Reading develops reading skills and expands vocabulary. The lesson opens with a *Before you read* exercise, whose purpose is to activate prior knowledge and encourage learners to make predictions. A *Reading tip*, which focuses learners on a specific reading skill, accompanies the *Read* exercise. The reading section of the lesson concludes with *After you read* exercises that check students' understanding. In the Basic Student's Book and Student's Books 1 and 2, the vocabulary expansion portion of the lesson is a *Picture dictionary*. It includes a *word bank*, pictures to identify, and a conversation for practicing the new words. The words are intended to expand vocabulary related to the unit topic. In Student's Books 3 and 4, the vocabulary expansion portion of the lesson occurs in *Check your understanding*.

LESSON E Writing provides writing practice within the context of the unit. There are three kinds of exercises in the lesson: prewriting, writing, and postwriting. *Before you write* exercises provide warm-up activities to activate the language students will need for the writing and one or more exercises that provide a model for students to follow when they write. A *Writing tip*, which presents information about punctuation or organization directly related to the writing assignment, accompanies the *Write* exercise. The Write exercise sets goals for the student writing. In the *After you write* exercise, students share with a partner using guided questions and the steps of the writing process.

LESSON F Another view has three sections.

- **Life-skills reading** develops the scanning and skimming skills that are used with documents such as forms, charts, schedules, announcements, and ads. Multiple-choice questions that follow the document develop test-taking skills similar to CASAS[2] and BEST.[3] This section concludes with an exercise that encourages student communication by providing questions that focus on some aspect of information in the document.
- **Fun with language** provides exercises that review and sometimes expand the topic, vocabulary, or grammar of the unit. They are interactive activities for partner or group work.
- **Wrap up** refers students to the self-assessment page in the back of the book, where they can check their knowledge and evaluate their progress.

The Author Team

Gretchen Bitterlin	Sylvia Ramirez
Dennis Johnson	K. Lynn Savage
Donna Price	

---

[2] The Comprehensive Adult Student Assessment System. For more information, see www.casas.org.

[3] The Basic English Skills Test. For more information, see www.cal.org/BEST.

Correlations

UNIT/PAGES	CASAS	EFF
Unit 1 **Personal information** pages 6–17	0.1.2, 0.1.4, 0.1.5, 0.1.6, 0.2.1, 0.2.3, 0.2.4, 1.1.6, 1.1.9, 1.2.1, 1.2.5, 1.3.1, 1.3.3, 1.3.4, 1.3.9, 1.6.4, 2.4.2, 2.6.1, 4.8.1, 4.8.2, 4.8.3, 6.0.2, 7.2.1, 7.4.7, 7.5.1, 8.1.2, 8.1.4	Most EFF standards are met, with particular focus on: • Conveying ideas in writing • Interacting with others in positive ways • Monitoring comprehension • Reading with understanding • Speaking so others can understand • Understanding and working with pictures
Unit 2 **At school** pages 18–29	0.1.2, 0.1.4, 0.1.5, 0.2.1, 0.2.4, 1.2.1, 1.9.6, 2.3.2, 2.5.5, 4.1.4, 4.1.6, 4.1.7, 4.1.8, 4.1.9, 4.4.2, 4.4.5, 4.8.1, 4.8.2, 7.1.1, 7.1.4, 7.2.2, 7.2.6, 7.3.1, 7.3.2, 7.3.4, 7.4.2, 7.4.7, 7.4.8, 7.5.1, 7.5.7, 8.3.2	Most EFF standards are met, with particular focus on: • Conveying ideas in writing • Guiding others • Listening actively • Paying attention to the conventions of written English • Seeking input from others • Solving problems and making decisions
Unit 3 **Friends and family** pages 32–43	0.1.2, 0.1.4, 0.1.5, 0.2.1, 0.2.4, 1.2.1, 1.2.2, 1.2.4, 1.2.5, 1.5.2, 2.1.4, 2.6.1, 4.8.1, 4.8.2, 4.8.4, 6.0.1, 6.0.2, 6.0.3, 6.0.4, 6.1.1, 6.1.3, 6.2.3, 6.5.1, 6.6.6, 7.1.4, 7.2.1, 7.2.7, 7.3.2, 7.4.2, 7.4.3, 7.4.7, 7.5.1, 8.1.2, 8.2.1, 8.2.2, 8.2.3, 8.2.4	Most EFF standards are met, with particular focus on: • Attending to oral information • Organizing and presenting written information • Paying attention to the conventions of spoken English • Selecting appropriate reading strategies • Solving problems using appropriate quantitative procedures • Speaking so others can understand
Unit 4 **Health** pages 44–55	0.1.2, 0.1.4, 0.1.5, 0.2.1, 1.2.5, 3.1.1, 3.2.1, 3.3.1, 3.3.2, 3.4.1, 3.4.2, 3.4.3, 3.5.9, 4.3.3, 4.8.1, 7.1.4, 7.2.1, 7.3.2, 7.4.2, 7.4.7	Most EFF standards are met, with particular focus on: • Conveying ideas in writing • Offering clear input • Seeking input from others • Speaking so others can understand • Taking stock of where one is • Understanding and working with numbers
Unit 5 **Around town** pages 58–69	0.1.2, 0.1.4, 0.1.5, 0.1.6, 0.2.1, 0.2.4, 2.2.1, 2.2.3, 2.2.4, 2.3.1, 4.8.1, 6.0.1, 6.0.2, 6.0.3, 6.0.4, 6.1.2, 6.6.6, 7.1.1, 7.4.2, 7.4.7	Most EFF standards are met, with particular focus on: • Conveying ideas in writing • Listening actively • Offering clear input • Organizing and presenting written information • Selecting appropriate reading strategies • Understanding and working with numbers and pictures

SCANS	BEST Plus Form A	BEST Form B
Most SCANS standards are met, with particular focus on: • Acquiring and evaluating information • Improving basic skills • Interpreting and communicating information • Participating as a member of a team • Practicing self-management	Overall test preparation is supported, with particular impact on the following items: Locator: W1, W7 Level 1: 4.2 Level 3: 4.1	Overall test preparation is supported, with particular impact on the following areas: • Oral interview • Personal information • Money and shopping • Writing notes
Most SCANS standards are met, with particular focus on: • Acquiring and evaluating information • Improving basic skills • Organizing and maintaining information • Solving problems • Teaching others	Overall test preparation is supported, with particular impact on the following items: Locator: W5 Level 1: 4.2 Level 2: 4.2 Level 3: 2.2, 2.3, 5.2	Overall test preparation is supported, with particular impact on the following areas: • Calendar • Employment and training • Oral interview • Personal information • Reading passages • Reading signs, ads, and notices • Writing notes
Most SCANS standards are met, with particular focus on: • Allocating money • Improving basic skills • Interpreting and communicating information • Participating as a member of a team • Practicing self-management	Overall test preparation is supported, with particular impact on the following items: Locator: W6 Level 1: 4 Level 3: 4	Overall test preparation is supported, with particular impact on the following areas: • Money and shopping • Numbers • Personal information • Reading signs, ads, and notices • Reading passages • Time • Writing notes
Most SCANS standards are met, with particular focus on: • Acquiring and evaluating information • Organizing and maintaining information • Practicing reasoning • Practicing self-management • Seeing things in the mind's eye	Overall test preparation is supported, with particular impact on the following items: Level 3: 1.2, 1.3	Overall test preparation is supported, with particular impact on the following areas: • Emergencies and safety • Health and parts of the body • Labels • Oral interview • Personal information • Reading signs, ads, and notices • Reading passages • Writing notes
Most SCANS standards are met, with particular focus on: • Improving basic skills • Interpreting and communicating information • Knowing how to learn • Participating as a member of a team • Teaching others	Overall test preparation is supported, with particular impact on the following items: Locator: W6, W7 Level 1: 3.1, 3.2, 3.3 Level 2: 2.1	Overall test preparation is supported, with particular impact on the following areas: • Oral interview • Personal information • Reading passages • Time/Numbers • Train schedule • Writing notes

UNIT/PAGES	CASAS	EFF
Unit 6 **Time** pages 70–81	0.1.2, 0.1.4, 0.1.5, 0.2.1, 0.2.3, 0.2.4, 2.3.1, 2.3.2, 2.7.2, 4.8.1, 5.3.1, 5.3.6, 6.0.1, 7.1.1, 7.2.1, 7.2.4, 7.2.7, 7.4.2, 7.4.3, 7.4.7, 7.4.8, 7.5.1	Most EFF standards are met, with particular focus on: • Conveying ideas in writing • Cooperating with others • Paying attention to the conventions of spoken English • Reading with understanding • Reflecting and evaluating • Understanding and working with numbers and pictures
Unit 7 **Shopping** pages 84–95	0.1.2, 0.1.4, 0.1.5, 0.2.1, 1.1.6, 1.2.1, 1.2.2, 1.4.1, 1.6.3, 4.8.1, 6.0.1, 6.0.2, 7.1.1, 7.2.3, 7.4.2, 7.4.7, 7.5.1, 8.1.4	Most EFF standards are met, with particular focus on: • Attending to oral information • Attending to visual sources of information • Identifying strengths and weaknesses as a learner • Making inferences, predictions, or judgments • Seeking feedback and revising accordingly • Taking responsibility for learning
Unit 8 **Work** pages 96–107	0.1.2, 0.1.4, 0.1.5, 0.2.1, 1.1.6, 2.3.1, 2.3.2, 4.1.2, 4.1.6, 4.1.8, 4.2.1, 4.4.3, 4.5.1, 4.8.1, 4.8.2, 6.0.1, 7.1.1, 7.1.4, 7.2.1, 7.2.3, 7.4.7, 7.5.1	Most EFF standards are met, with particular focus on: • Listening actively • Monitoring comprehension and adjusting reading strategies • Organizing and presenting written information • Setting and prioritizing goals • Speaking so others can understand • Testing out new learning in real-life applications
Unit 9 **Daily living** pages 110–121	0.1.2, 0.1.4, 0.1.5, 0.2.1, 0.2.3, 1.1.6, 1.4.1, 1.4.5, 1.4.7, 1.6.3, 1.7.4, 1.7.5, 4.1.8, 4.8.1, 4.8.6, 6.0.1, 7.1.1, 7.1.2, 7.2.1, 7.2.2, 7.3.2, 7.3.4, 7.4.2, 7.4.7, 7.5.1, 7.5.6, 8.1.4, 8.2.6, 8.3.1, 8.3.2	Most EFF standards are met, with particular focus on: • Anticipating and identifying problems • Conveying ideas in writing • Engaging parties in trying to reach agreement • Reading with understanding • Setting and prioritizing goals • Speaking so others can understand
Unit 10 **Leisure** pages 122–133	0.1.2, 0.1.4, 0.1.5, 0.2.1, 0.2.3, 0.2.4, 2.3.1, 2.3.2, 2.6.1, 2.7.1, 2.7.2, 4.8.1, 4.8.3, 7.1.1, 7.2.1, 7.4.7, 7.5.1, 7.5.6	Most EFF standards are met, with particular focus on: • Cooperating with others • Identifying strengths and weaknesses as a learner • Paying attention to the conventions of spoken English • Reflecting and evaluating • Testing out new learning in real-life applications • Understanding and working with pictures and numbers

SCANS	BEST Plus Form A	BEST Form B
Most SCANS standards are met, with particular focus on: • Improving basic skills • Interpreting and communicating information • Knowing how to learn • Organizing and maintaining information • Participating as a member of a team	Overall test preparation is supported, with particular impact on the following items: Level 1: 4.1, 4.2 Level 3: 4.1	Overall test preparation is supported, with particular impact on the following areas: • Calendar • Oral interview • Personal information • Reading passages • Time/Numbers • Writing notes
Most SCANS standards are met, with particular focus on: • Acquiring and evaluating information • Interpreting and communicating information • Knowing how to learn • Participating as a member of a team • Practicing self-management	Overall test preparation is supported, with particular impact on the following items: Level 1: 2.1, 2.3 Level 2: 3.2 Level 3: 2.2	Overall test preparation is supported, with particular impact on the following areas: • Money and shopping • Oral interview • Personal information • Reading signs, ads, and notices • Reading passages • Writing notes
Most SCANS standards are met, with particular focus on: • Acquiring and evaluating information • Improving basic skills • Knowing how to learn • Practicing reasoning • Teaching others	Overall test preparation is supported, with particular impact on the following items: Locator: W5, W6	Overall test preparation is supported, with particular impact on the following areas: • Calendar • Employment and training • Oral interview • Personal information • Reading passages • Time/Numbers • Writing notes
Most SCANS standards are met, with particular focus on: • Improving basic skills • Practicing negotiation • Seeing things in the mind's eye • Serving clients and customers • Understanding systems	Overall test preparation is supported, with particular impact on the following items: Locator: W2 Level 1: 2.1, 2.2, 2.3 Level 2: 1.1, 3.1, 3.2 Level 3: 2.2, 2.3	Overall test preparation is supported, with particular impact on the following areas: • Emergencies and safety • Housing • Oral interview • Personal information • Reading signs, ads, and notices • Reading passages • Time/Numbers • Writing notes
Most SCANS standards are met, with particular focus on: • Improving basic skills • Knowing how to learn • Participating as a member of a team • Practicing sociability • Teaching others • Working with diversity	Overall test preparation is supported, with particular impact on the following items: Locator: W7 Level 1: 4.1, 4.2 Level 3: 1.1, 4.1	Overall test preparation is supported, with particular impact on the following areas: • Calendar • Oral interview • Personal information • Reading passages • Time/Numbers • Writing notes

Meet the Ventures author team

Gretchen Bitterlin has been an ESL instructor and ESL department instructional leader with the Continuing Education Program, San Diego Community College District. She now coordinates that agency's large noncredit ESL program. She was also an ESL Teacher Institute Trainer and Chair of the TESOL Task Force on Adult Education Program Standards. She is a co-author of *English for Adult Competency*.

Dennis Johnson has been an ESL instructor at City College of San Francisco, teaching all levels of ESL, since 1977. As ESL Site Coordinator, he has provided guidance to faculty in selecting textbooks. He is the author of *Get Up and Go* and co-author of *The Immigrant Experience*.

Donna Price is Associate Professor of ESL and Vocational ESL/Technology Resource Instructor for the Continuing Education Program, San Diego Community College District. She has taught all levels of ESL for 20 years and is a former recipient of the TESOL Newbury House Award for Excellence in Teaching. She is also the author of *Skills for Success*.

Sylvia Ramirez is a professor at MiraCosta College, where she coordinates the large noncredit ESL program. She has more than 30 years of experience in adult ESL, including multilevel ESL, vocational ESL, family literacy, and distance learning. She has represented the California State Department of Education in providing technical assistance to local ESL programs.

K. Lynn Savage, Series Editor, is a retired ESL teacher and Vocational ESL Resource teacher from City College of San Francisco, who trains teachers for adult education programs around the country. She chaired the committee that developed *ESL Model Standards for Adult Education Programs* (California, 1992) and is the author, co-author, and editor of many ESL materials including *Teacher Training through Video*, *Parenting for Academic Success: A Curriculum for Families Learning English*, *Crossroads Café*, *Building Life Skills*, *Picture Stories*, *May I Help You?*, and *English That Works*.

To the student

Welcome to *Ventures 2*! We want you to enjoy using your *Ventures* Student's Book in your classroom. We also hope that you will use this book to study on your own. For that reason, the Student's Book comes with an audio CD. Use it at home to review and practice the material you are learning in class. You will make faster progress in learning English if you take the time to study at home and do your homework.

Good luck in your studies!

The Author Team
Gretchen Bitterlin
Dennis Johnson
Donna Price
Sylvia Ramirez
K. Lynn Savage

Welcome

1 Meet your classmates

A Look at the picture. What do you see?
B What are the people doing?

2 Greetings and introductions

A **Read** the conversations. Complete the sentences with words from the box.

address	date of birth	last name	name
apartment	home phone	middle initial	zip code

1. **A** What's your ___name___?
   B Ben Navarro.

2. **A** How do you spell your
   ___last name___?
   B N-A-V-A-R-R-O.

3. **A** Do you have a
   ___middle Initial___?
   B Yes. It's *J*.

4. **A** What's your
   ___address___?
   B 1737 Van Dam Street, Brooklyn, New York.

5. **A** What's your ___zip code___?
   B It's 11222.

6. **A** Do you have an ___apartment___ number?
   B Yes. It's 3A.

7. **A** What's your ___home phone___ number?
   B 718-555-5983.

8. **A** What's your ___date of birth___?
   B January 18th, 1982.

SELF-STUDY AUDIO CD

Listen and check your answers. Then practice with a partner.

B **Talk** with a partner. Ask questions. Write your partner's answers.

What's your first name?   Ben.

Library Card Application

Ben	J.	Navarro
First name	Middle initial	Last name

1737 Van Dam street.	3A.
Address	Apartment number

Brooklyn	New york	11222
City	State	Zip code

718-555-5983	01/18/1982
Home phone	Date of birth

Talk with your class. Introduce your partner.

This is my classmate Ben Navarro. His birthday is January 18th.   Nice to meet you, Ben.

3 Verb tense review

A Listen to each sentence. Complete the chart. Check (✓) the time words.

	Now	Every day	Yesterday	Tomorrow
1.		✓		
2.				
3.				
4.				
5.				

Listen again. Check your answers.

B Read about Stefan's day. Complete the story. Use the correct verb tense.

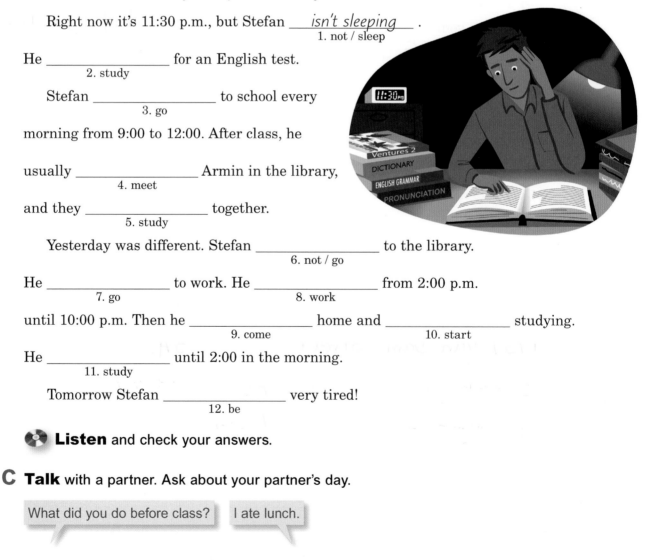

Right now it's 11:30 p.m., but Stefan ___*isn't sleeping*___ .
1. not / sleep

He _____ for an English test.
2. study

Stefan _____ to school every
3. go

morning from 9:00 to 12:00. After class, he

usually _____ Armin in the library,
4. meet

and they _____ together.
5. study

Yesterday was different. Stefan _____ to the library.
6. not / go

He _____ to work. He _____ from 2:00 p.m.
7. go   8. work

until 10:00 p.m. Then he _____ home and _____ studying.
9. come   10. start

He _____ until 2:00 in the morning.
11. study

Tomorrow Stefan _____ very tired!
12. be

SELF-STUDY AUDIO CD

Listen and check your answers.

C Talk with a partner. Ask about your partner's day.

What did you do before class?   I ate lunch.

4 Work skills and life skills

A **Listen.** Soon Mi is at the library. She is talking about her work skills. Check (✓) the things Soon Mi can do.

✓ use a computer   ____ read to children   ____ write in English

____ speak English   ____ speak Spanish   ____ speak Korean

Talk with a partner. What work skills do you have? What work skills are you going to learn?

> I can use a computer.

> I can't use a computer, but I'm going to learn.

B **Talk** about life skills with your classmates. Complete the chart.

> Armin, can you swim?

> Yes, I can.

Find a classmate who can:	Classmate's name
swim	Armin
iron a shirt	
cook	
drive a truck	
paint a house	
speak three languages	

Useful language
How do you spell that?

Talk with your class. Ask and answer questions.

> Who can swim?

> Armin can.

> Ali can, too.

C **Read** the list. Check (✓) the things you can do. Add two more skills.

Things I can do in English

☐ introduce myself
☐ say my address and telephone number
☐ register for a class
☐ make an appointment with a doctor
☐ give directions
☐ write a shopping list
☐ ask about prices

☐ help my child with homework
☐ read to my child
☐ read a class schedule
☐ read a television schedule
☐ talk about my weekend
_____
_____

Talk with a partner. Share your information.

Lesson A *Get ready*

1 Talk about the picture

A Look at the picture. What do you see?

B Point to: long brown hair • straight hair • black shoes • a soccer uniform
curly blond hair • short black hair • a red shirt • a striped skirt

C Describe the people. What are they doing?

2 Listening

  A 🔊 **Listen.** Who is Shoko talking about? Write the letter of the conversation.

1. ____

2. *a*

3. ____

  B 🔊 **Listen again.** Write *T* (true) or *F* (false).

Conversation A

1. Victoria is Shoko's daughter.   *T*

2. Victoria plays soccer every day.   ____

3. Victoria looks like her mother.   ____

Conversation B

4. Eddie is Shoko's brother.   ____

5. Eddie is playing computer games.   ____

6. Eddie is a very quiet boy.   ____

Conversation C

7. Mark is Shoko's husband.   ____

8. Mark wears small shirts and pants.   ____

9. Mark studies Spanish.   ____

Listen again. Check your answers.

C **Talk** with a partner. Describe someone in your family.

> My mother has long blond hair.

> My mother has curly brown hair.

She's wearing a short plaid skirt.

1 Grammar focus: adjective order

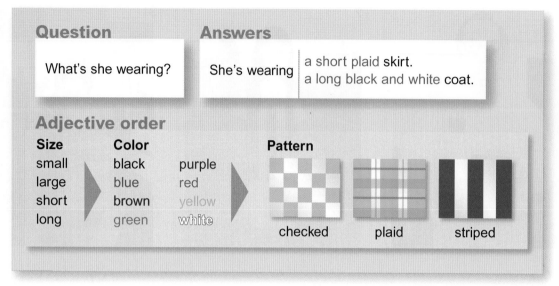

2 Practice

A Write. Complete the conversations. Write the words in the correct order.

1. **A** What's Amy wearing?

   B She's wearing a _____*long*_____ _____*black*_____ dress.

(black / long)

2. **A** What's she wearing?

   B She's wearing _____ _____ pants.

(black and white / checked)

3. **A** What does he take to school?

   B He takes a _____ _____ backpack.

(large / red)

4. **A** What do you usually wear to work?

   B I wear a _____ _____ uniform.

(blue and white / striped)

5. **A** What's he wearing today?

   B He's wearing a _____ _____ sweater.

(plaid / red and yellow)

6. **A** What are they wearing?

   B They're wearing _____ _____ skirts.

(green / short)

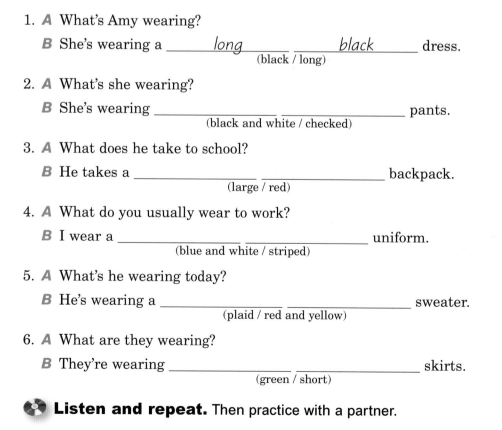 **Listen and repeat.** Then practice with a partner.

B Write the letter. What are the people wearing?

a. blue plaid pants   f. long black boots
b. a long purple coat   g. a long yellow shirt
c. small red shoes   h. red and white striped socks
d. a blue checked skirt   i. a big brown sweater
e. a short striped dress   j. a green plaid suit

1. _g_
2. _____
3. _____
4. _____
5. _____
6. _____
7. _____
8. _____
9. _____
10. _____

Lisa   Luis   Nick   Gina

Talk with a partner. Change the **bold** words and make conversations.

A What's **Lisa** wearing?
B **She's** wearing **a long yellow shirt**.

Useful language
Some clothing items are always plural:
jeans, pants, shorts

3 Communicate

Talk with a partner about your classmates.

What's Maya wearing?   She's wearing jeans and a long green sweater.

What are you doing right now?

1 Grammar focus: present continuous and simple present

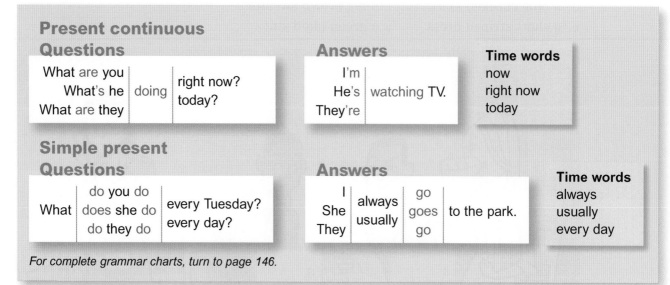

Present continuous

Questions

What are you		right now?
What's he	doing	
What are they		today?

Answers

I'm	
He's	watching TV.
They're	

Time words
now
right now
today

Simple present

Questions

What	do you do	every Tuesday?
	does she do	
	do they do	every day?

Answers

I		go	
She	always	goes	to the park.
They	usually	go	

Time words
always
usually
every day

For complete grammar charts, turn to page 146.

2 Practice

A Write. Complete the conversations. Use the correct form of the verb.

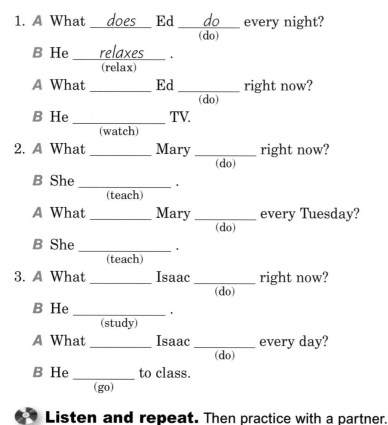

1. **A** What ___does___ Ed ___do___ every night?
   (do)

   B He ___relaxes___ .
   (relax)

   A What _____ Ed _____ right now?
   (do)

   B He _____ TV.
   (watch)

2. **A** What _____ Mary _____ right now?
   (do)

   B She _____ .
   (teach)

   A What _____ Mary _____ every Tuesday?
   (do)

   B She _____ .
   (teach)

3. **A** What _____ Isaac _____ right now?
   (do)

   B He _____ .
   (study)

   A What _____ Isaac _____ every day?
   (do)

   B He _____ to class.
   (go)

Listen and repeat. Then practice with a partner.

B **Talk** with a partner. Change the **bold** words and make conversations.

> **A** Look! **Betty is leaving early!**
> **B** Of course. **She leaves early** every night.

1. Betty / leave early
2. Henry / call his wife
3. Jin Ho / study alone
4. Olga and Yuri / speak English
5. Yan and Ling / drink coffee
6. Antonio / wear jeans and a tie

3 Communicate

A **Talk** with a partner. Ask and answer questions about your habits.

> **A** What do you do on the weekend?
> **B** I always do things with my children.

> **A** What do you do every night?
> **B** I usually study English.

B **Talk** in a group. Ask and answer questions about your classmates right now.

> **A** What's Sara doing right now?
> **B** She's talking to Samuel and Kwan.

Lesson D Reading

1 Before you read

Look at the picture. Answer the questions.

1. Who is the girl?
2. What is she wearing?
3. What is she doing?

2 Read

SELF-STUDY AUDIO CD **Read** Shoko's e-mail. Listen and read again.

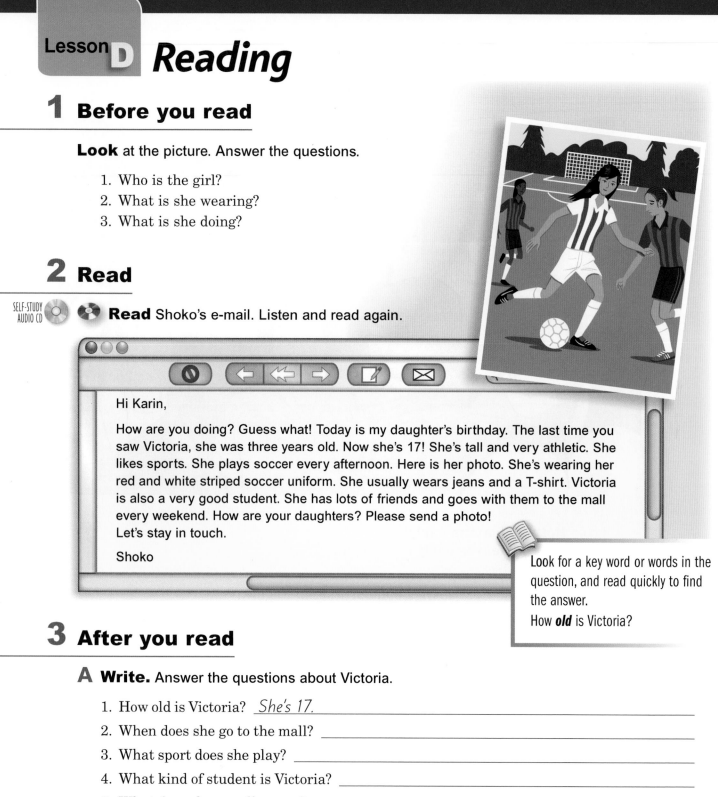

Hi Karin,

How are you doing? Guess what! Today is my daughter's birthday. The last time you saw Victoria, she was three years old. Now she's 17! She's tall and very athletic. She likes sports. She plays soccer every afternoon. Here is her photo. She's wearing her red and white striped soccer uniform. She usually wears jeans and a T-shirt. Victoria is also a very good student. She has lots of friends and goes with them to the mall every weekend. How are your daughters? Please send a photo!
Let's stay in touch.

Shoko

Look for a key word or words in the question, and read quickly to find the answer.
How **old** is Victoria?

3 After you read

A Write. Answer the questions about Victoria.

1. How old is Victoria? _She's 17._
2. When does she go to the mall? _____
3. What sport does she play? _____
4. What kind of student is Victoria? _____
5. What does she usually wear? _____

B Write. Complete the sentences about Victoria.

1. Victoria is very ___athletic___ .
2. She likes _____ .
3. She has lots of _____ .
4. She's wearing _____ .

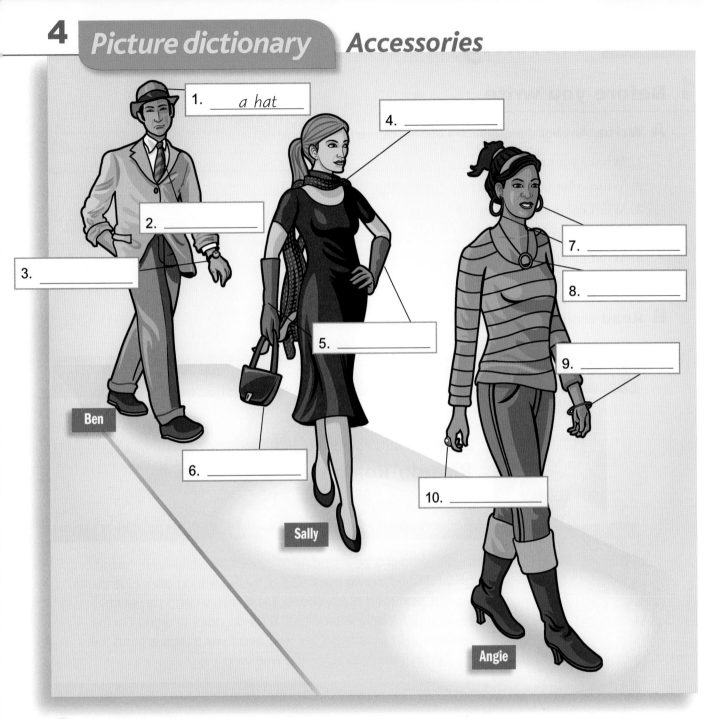

1. ___a hat___
2. _____
3. _____
4. _____
5. _____
6. _____
7. _____
8. _____
9. _____
10. _____

Ben

Sally

Angie

SELF-STUDY
AUDIO CD

A **Write** the words in the picture dictionary. Then listen and repeat.

| a bracelet | gloves | a necklace | a ring | a tie |
| earrings | a hat | a purse | a scarf | a watch |

B **Talk** with a partner. Change the **bold** words and make conversations.

A What's Ben wearing?
B He's wearing **a red and green striped tie**.

A What's Sally wearing?
B She's wearing **a green and black checked scarf**.

1 Before you write

A Write. Answer the questions about yourself.

1. What's your name? _____
2. What color is your hair? _____
3. What color are your eyes? _____
4. What are you wearing? _____
5. What do you do after class? _____
6. What do you do on the weekend? _____

B Read about a new classmate.

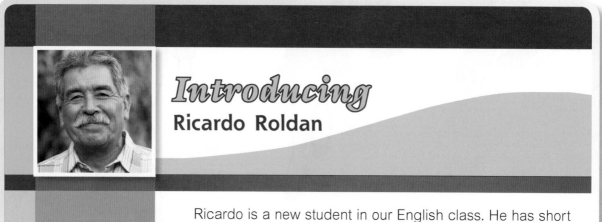

Introducing
Ricardo Roldan

Ricardo is a new student in our English class. He has short gray hair and brown eyes. Today he is wearing dark blue pants, a plaid shirt, and black shoes. He is also wearing a watch. He is very friendly. After class, Ricardo goes to work. On the weekend, Ricardo helps his wife and fixes things around the house. He also relaxes on the weekend.

C Write. Answer the questions about Ricardo.

1. Does Ricardo have gray hair or brown hair? *Gray hair.* _____
2. Is his hair long or short? _____
3. What is he wearing? _____
4. What does he do on the weekend? _____

D Write each sentence in a different way.

1. After class, Ricardo goes to work.

   Ricardo goes to work after class.

2. Tanya goes shopping on the weekend.

   _____

3. Victoria plays soccer every Tuesday.

   _____

4. After work, Henry watches TV.

   _____

5. On the weekend, Yan studies English.

   _____

Time phrases like *after class* or *on the weekend* can come at the beginning or end of a sentence. Use a comma if they are at the beginning.

E Talk with a partner. Complete the chart. Use the questions in Exercise 1A.

Partner's name:	
Hair color:	
Eye color:	
Clothing:	
Accessories:	
After-class activities:	
Weekend activities:	

2 Write

Write a paragraph about your partner. Use Exercises 1B and 1E to help you.

3 After you write

A Read your paragraph to your partner.

B Check your partner's paragraph.
- What did your partner write about you?
- Is the information correct?
- Are the time phrases correct?

Another view

1 Life-skills reading

ORDER FORM

ITEM NUMBER	QUANTITY	SIZE	COLOR	ITEM NAME	PRICE
105B	1	L	RED	SWEATER	$29.00
265A	1	M	PURPLE	COAT	$69.00
350G	2	XS	WHITE	T-SHIRT	$18.00
670F	1	8	BLACK	SHOES	$59.00

METHOD OF PAYMENT:

- ☐ Global Express
- ☑ MasterCharge
- ☐ Vista
- ☐ Discovery
- ☐ Personal check

CREDIT CARD ACCOUNT NUMBER:

123-1234-123

EXPIRATION DATE:

12/2010

SIGNATURE:

Phong Nguyen

SUBTOTAL	$175.00
SHIPPING AND HANDLING	$15.00

Under $50.........$5.00
$50–$100............$10.00
Over $100.........$15.00

EXPRESS DELIVERY

(ADD $5.00)

TOTAL $190.00

Useful language

XS	extra small
S	small
M	medium
L	large
XL	extra large

A Read the questions. Look at the order form. Circle the answers.

1. How much is the large red sweater?
   a. $18.00
   b. $29.00
   c. $59.00
   d. $69.00

2. What color are the shoes?
   a. black
   b. purple
   c. red
   d. white

3. What is the method of payment?
   a. Discovery
   b. Global Express
   c. MasterCharge
   d. Vista

4. How much is shipping and handling?
   a. $5.00
   b. $10.00
   c. $15.00
   d. $150.00

B Talk in a group. Ask and answer the questions.

1. Where do you shop for clothing?
2. What clothes do you usually buy?
3. How do you usually pay?

2 Fun with language

A Work in a group. Talk about the ways Bob and Louise are different. Write your ideas in the chart.

Bob

He has blue eyes.

Louise

She has green eyes.

B Work in a group. Play a game. Sit in a circle. One person describes a student. Everyone tries to guess who it is.

She's wearing blue pants and a striped shirt.

Is it Soon Mi?

3 Wrap up

Complete the **Self-assessment** on page 141.

Lesson A *Get ready*

1 Talk about the picture

A Look at the picture. What do you see?

B Point to: an English teacher • a computer lab • a hall • a monitor
a lab instructor • an ESL classroom • a keyboard • a mouse

C Look at the people. What are they doing?

2 Listening

A 🔊 **Listen.** Who is Joseph talking to? Write the letter of the conversation.

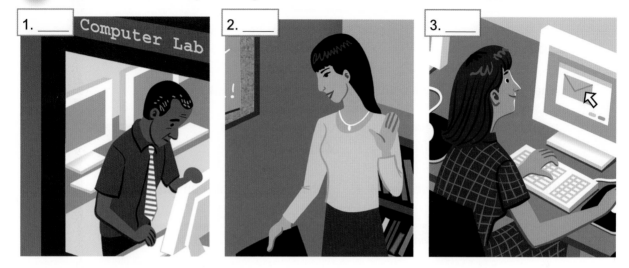

1. ____ Computer Lab
2. ____
3. ____

B 🔊 **Listen again.** Write *T* (true) or *F* (false).

Conversation A

1. Eva and Joseph are in the computer lab. _F_

2. Mrs. Lee helped Eva. ____

3. Joseph is taking a keyboarding class. ____

Conversation B

4. Joseph needs to use a computer at work. ____

5. The computer lab is next door to Joseph's classroom. ____

6. Mrs. Lee is the lab instructor. ____

Conversation C

7. Joseph needs to register for a keyboarding class. ____

8. Mrs. Smith works in the computer lab. ____

9. Joseph needs to register next month. ____

Listen again. Check your answers.

C **Talk** with a partner. Ask and answer the questions.

1. What are some important skills?
2. What new skills do you want to learn?

Lesson B *What do you want to do?*

1 Grammar focus: *want* and *need*

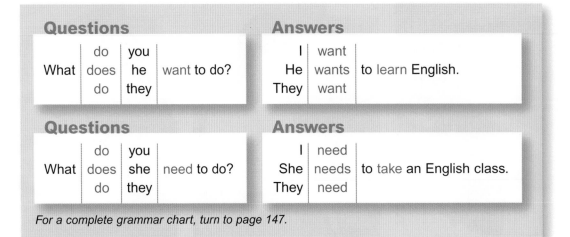

Questions				Answers		
What	do does do	you he they	want to do?	I He They	want wants want	to learn English.

Questions				Answers		
What	do does do	you she they	need to do?	I She They	need needs need	to take an English class.

For a complete grammar chart, turn to page 147.

2 Practice

A Write. Complete the conversations.

1. **A** What do you want to do now?

   B I ___*want to get*___ my GED.

(want / get)

2. **A** What do you need to do?

   B I _____ a GED class.

(need / take)

3. **A** What does Sandra want to do this year?

   B She _____ about computers.

(want / learn)

4. **A** What does Ali want to do this year?

   B He _____ more money.

(want / make)

5. **A** What does Celia need to do tonight?

   B She _____ her homework.

(need / do)

6. **A** What do Sergio and Elena want to do next year?

   B They _____ citizens.

(want / become)

> **Culture note**
> The GED (General Educational Development) is a certificate. It is equal to a high school diploma.

Listen and repeat. Then practice with a partner.

B Talk with a partner. Change the **bold** words and make conversations.

> **A** **She wants** to **fix cars**. What **does she** need to do?
> **B** **She needs** to **study auto mechanics**.
> **A** That's a good idea.

she / fix cars
study auto mechanics

they / learn computer skills
take a computer class

he / make more money
get a second job

he / get a driver's license
take driving lessons

they / become citizens
take a citizenship class

she / go to college
talk to a counselor

3 Communicate

Talk with your classmates. Ask about their goals. Give advice.

What do you want to do?   I want to get a good job.

Why don't you take a computer class?

Useful language

Why don't you take a computer class?
You could take a computer class.

Lesson C *What will you do?*

1 Grammar focus: future with *will*

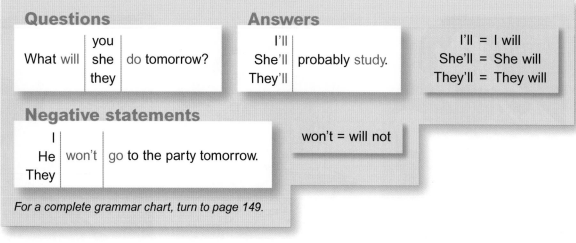

Questions

| What will | you she they | do tomorrow? |

Answers

| I'll She'll They'll | probably study. |

I'll = I will
She'll = She will
They'll = They will

Negative statements

| I He They | won't | go to the party tomorrow. |

won't = will not

For a complete grammar chart, turn to page 149.

2 Practice

A Write. Complete the sentences. Use *will* or *won't*.

1
~~Emily's party tonight 7:30 p.m.~~
Study for test.

2
Volunteer in Tom's class
on ~~Tuesday~~, 10:00 a.m.
Wednesday

3
Work on ~~Wednesday~~ afternoon.
Thursday

4
Talk to college counselor
on ~~Thursday~~.
Friday

1. Sue has a test tomorrow. She __will__ study tonight. She __won't__ go to the party.

2. She _____ volunteer in Tom's class on Wednesday. She _____ volunteer on Tuesday.

3. She _____ work on Wednesday afternoon. She _____ work on Thursday.

4. She _____ talk to a counselor on Thursday. She _____ talk to a counselor on Friday.

Listen and repeat. Check your answers.

B **Talk** with a partner. Change the **bold** words and make conversations.

> **A** What will you do in the next five years?
> **B** Maybe I'll **open a business**.
> **A** That's great!

open a business

take a vocational course

start business school

go to college

learn a new language

buy a house

3 Communicate

Talk with your classmates. Ask and answer questions about future plans.

> **A** Ming, what will you do next year?
> **B** I'll probably take a vocational course.
> **A** What will you do after that?
> **B** Maybe I'll get a new job. I want to make more money.

Lesson D Reading

1 Before you read

Look at the picture. Answer the questions.

1. Who is the man?
2. Where is he?

2 Read

SELF-STUDY
AUDIO CD

Read Joseph's application. Listen and read again.

What are your future goals? What steps do you need to take?

I want to open my own electronics store. I need to take three steps to reach my goal. First, I need to learn keyboarding. Second, I need to take business classes. Third, I need to work in an electronics store. I will probably open my store in a couple of years.

> First, read quickly to get the main idea. Ask yourself *What is it about?*

3 After you read

A Write. Answer the questions about Joseph.

1. What is Joseph's goal? _He wants to open his own electronics store._
2. What does he need to do first? _____
3. What does he need to do second? _____
4. What does he need to do after that? _____
5. When will he open his business? _____

B Write. Complete the sentences.

business	electronics	goal	learn	steps

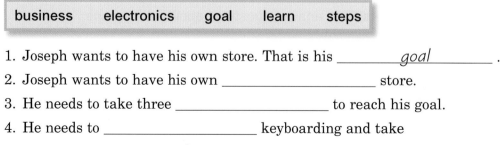

1. Joseph wants to have his own store. That is his _____ _goal_ _____ .
2. Joseph wants to have his own _____ store.
3. He needs to take three _____ to reach his goal.
4. He needs to _____ keyboarding and take _____ classes.

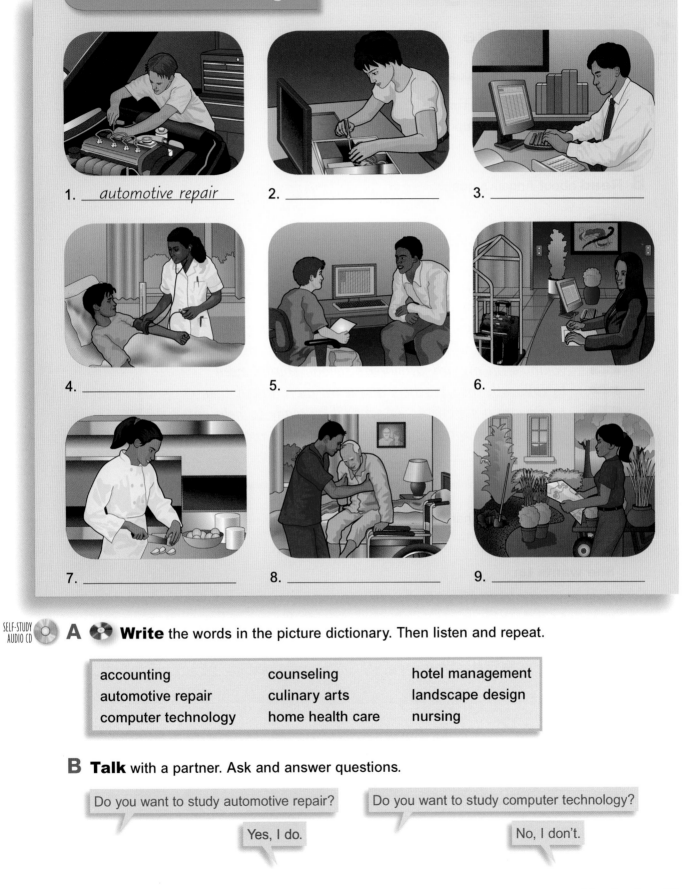

1. ___automotive repair___

2. _____

3. _____

4. _____

5. _____

6. _____

7. _____

8. _____

9. _____

SELF-STUDY AUDIO CD

A **Write** the words in the picture dictionary. Then listen and repeat.

accounting	counseling	hotel management
automotive repair	culinary arts	landscape design
computer technology	home health care	nursing

B **Talk** with a partner. Ask and answer questions.

Do you want to study automotive repair?

Yes, I do.

Do you want to study computer technology?

No, I don't.

Lesson E *Writing*

1 Before you write

A Talk with a partner. Ask and answer the questions.

1. What are your goals this year?
2. What is your most important goal? Why?
3. What do you need to do to reach your goal?

B Read about Angela's goal.

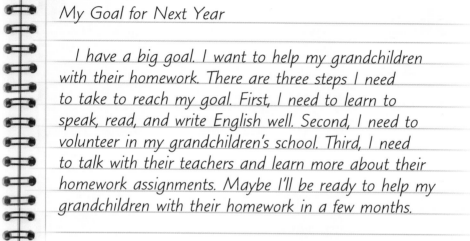

My Goal for Next Year

    I have a big goal. I want to help my grandchildren with their homework. There are three steps I need to take to reach my goal. First, I need to learn to speak, read, and write English well. Second, I need to volunteer in my grandchildren's school. Third, I need to talk with their teachers and learn more about their homework assignments. Maybe I'll be ready to help my grandchildren with their homework in a few months.

C Write. Complete the chart about Angela's goal.

Angela's goal

She wants to:
help her grandchildren with their homework
She needs to:
1.
2.
3.
She will probably reach her goal in:

D Read Donald's chart. Talk with a partner. Ask and answer.

1. What does Donald want to do?
2. First, what does he need to do?
3. Second, what does he need to do?
4. Third, what does he need to do?
5. When will he probably reach his goal?

Donald's goal

I want to:
get a job as a landscape designer
I need to:
1. *work in people's gardens*
2. *take a course in landscape design*
3. *look for jobs in the newspaper*
I will probably reach my goal in:
two years

E Write. Complete the chart about your goal.

My goal

I want to:
I need to:
1.
2.
3.
I will probably reach my goal in:

2 Write

Write a paragraph about your goal. Write about the steps
you need to take. Use Exercises 1B, 1D, and 1E to help you.

3 After you write

A Read your paragraph to a partner.

B Check your partner's paragraph.

• What is your partner's goal?
• What are the three steps?
• Did your partner use the words *First, Second,* and *Third*?

Begin sentences with words
like *First, Second,* and *Third*
to organize your ideas.

Another view

1 Life-skills reading

COURSE CATALOG

General Equivalency Diploma (GED)

Do you want to get your GED? Then you need to practice your reading, writing, and math skills. Classes are in English or Spanish. No fee.

Instructor: Mr. Chen (English)
            Ms. Lopez (Spanish)
Days/Times: Mon, Wed 6:00 p.m.–8:00 p.m.

TV and DVD Repair

This class will teach you how to repair TVs and DVD players. You will also learn about opening your own repair shop. Fee: $85

Instructor: Mr. Stern
Days/Times: Mon, Tues 6:00 p.m.– 8:00 p.m.

Introduction to Computers

This class is for adults who want to learn about computers and the Internet. You will learn about keyboarding, e-mail, and computer jobs. Fee: $75

Instructor: Mrs. Gates
Days/Times: Mon, Wed 7:00 p.m.–9:00 p.m.

Citizenship

Do you want to be an American citizen? First, you need to learn about American history and civics. This class will prepare you for the U.S. citizenship test. Requirements: Legal resident. No fee.

Instructor: Ms. Cuevas
Days/Times: Thurs 7:00 p.m.–9:00 p.m.

A Read the questions. Look at the course catalog. Circle the answers.

1. How much will the GED class cost?
   a. $35
   b. $75
   c. $85
   d. no fee

2. When is the computer class?
   a. Monday and Tuesday
   b. Monday and Wednesday
   c. Tuesday and Thursday
   d. Wednesday and Friday

3. Who will teach TV and DVD Repair?
   a. Mr. Chen
   b. Ms. Cuevas
   c. Mrs. Gates
   d. Mr. Stern

4. Which class is in English or Spanish?
   a. Citizenship
   b. GED
   c. Introduction to Computers
   d. TV and DVD Repair

B Talk with a partner. Ask and answer the questions.

1. What do you want to learn about this year?
2. What classes will you take?

2 Fun with language

A Work with a partner. Match the courses with the pictures.

accounting	culinary arts	landscape design
automotive repair	hotel management	nursing

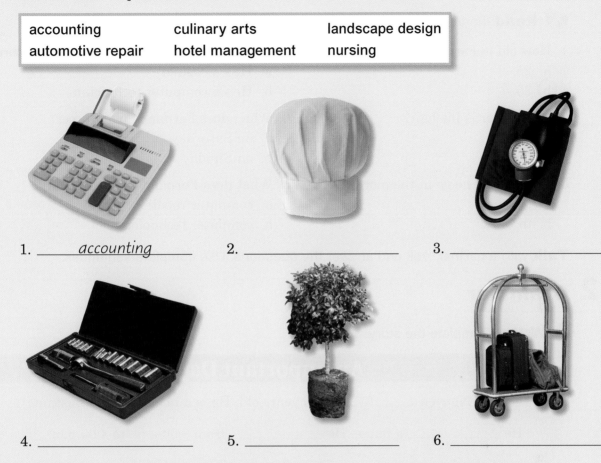

1. _accounting_

2. _____

3. _____

4. _____

5. _____

6. _____

B Work in a group. Play a game. Sit in a circle. The first person says one goal. The next person repeats the first goal and adds another goal. Continue until everyone has a chance to speak.

I want to find a new job.

Maria wants to find a new job. I want to buy a house.

3 Wrap up

Complete the **Self-assessment** on page 141.

Review

1 Listening

Read the questions. Then listen and circle the answers.

1. How old is Fernando?
   a. 25
   (b.) 35

2. What color is his hair?
   a. brown
   b. black

3. Where does he go in the morning?
   a. to school
   b. to work

4. What does he do at Green's Grocery Store?
   a. He's a cashier.
   b. He's a computer technician.

5. When does Fernando play soccer?
   a. on Saturday
   b. on Sunday

6. What does Fernando want to study?
   a. computer repair
   b. computer technology

Talk with a partner. Ask and answer the questions. Use complete sentences.

2 Grammar

A Write. Complete the story.

An Important Day

Tan Nguyen _____*is*_____ 45 years old. He is a home health assistant.
                    1. be

He _____ a nurse. He _____ from 8:00 a.m. to 4:00 p.m.,
      2. want / be   3. work

but today he _____ . This afternoon, he and his wife _____
               4. not / work   5. become

United States citizens. Every day at work, Tan _____ a uniform.
                                                    6. wear

Today he _____ a new blue suit, a white shirt, and a red and white
          7. wear

striped tie. Tan is very excited.

B Write. Look at the answers. Write the questions.

1. **A** How old _is Tan_ ?
   B Tan is 45 years old.

2. **A** What _____ ?
   B He is a home health assistant.

3. **A** When _____ ?
   B He usually works from 8:00 a.m. to 4:00 p.m.

4. **A** What _____ ?
   B Today he is wearing a blue suit, a white shirt, and a striped tie.

Talk with a partner. Ask and answer the questions.

3 Pronunciation: strong syllables

A 🔊 **Listen** to the syllables in these words.

pȧper   rėstaurant   compůter

B 🔊 **Listen and repeat.** Clap for each syllable. Clap loudly for the strong syllable.

● ●	● ●	● ● ●	● ● ●	● ● ● ●
necklace	cashier	medium	mechanic	television
nursing	career	counselor	accounting	citizenship
bracelet	repair	uniform	tomorrow	usually
sweater	achieve	manager	computer	
jacket		citizen	eraser	

Talk with a partner. Take turns. Say each word. Your partner claps for each syllable.

C 🔊 **Listen** for the strong syllable in each word. Put a circle over the strong syllable.

1. instrúctor   4. dictionary   7. management
2. uniform   5. business   8. landscape
3. sweatshirt   6. enroll   9. design

D **Write** eight words from Units 1 and 2. Put a circle over the strong syllable in each word.

1.	5.
2.	6.
3.	7.
4.	8.

Talk with a partner. Read the words.

1 Talk about the picture

A Look at the picture. What do you see?

B Point to: a broken-down car • smoke • groceries • a trunk
a cell phone • an engine • a supermarket • a hood

C Look at the people. What happened?

Friends and family

Rosa

2 Listening

A **Listen.** Who is Rosa talking to? Write the letter of the conversation.

1. _____

2. _____

3. _____

B **Listen again.** Write *T* (true) or *F* (false).

Conversation A

1. Rosa went to the supermarket with her friends.   *F*

2. Rosa's car broke down.   _____

3. Rosa opened the hood of the car.   _____

Conversation B

4. Mike works at a coffee shop.   _____

5. Rosa bought groceries for a picnic.   _____

6. Mike will pick up Rosa and her children.   _____

Conversation C

7. Ling needs a ride to school tonight.   _____

8. Rosa usually leaves her house at 7:00.   _____

9. Ling will pick up Rosa at 8:00.   _____

Listen again. Check your answers.

C **Talk** with a partner. Ask and answer the questions.

1. Did you ever ask a friend for help?
2. Did a friend or family member ever ask you for help?
3. What happened?

What did you do last weekend?

1 Grammar focus: simple past with regular and irregular verbs

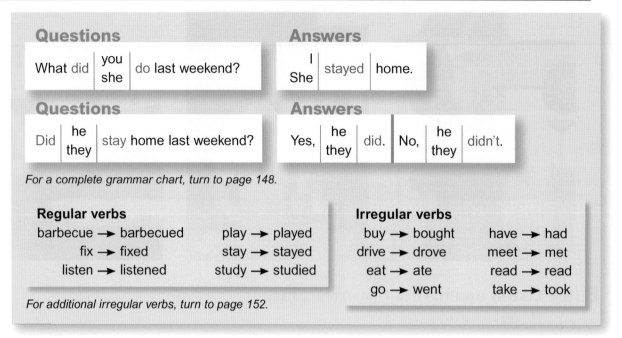

Questions

What did	you she	do last weekend?

Answers

I She	stayed	home.

Questions

Did	he they	stay home last weekend?

Answers

Yes,	he they	did.	No,	he they	didn't.

For a complete grammar chart, turn to page 148.

Regular verbs

barbecue → barbecued   play → played
fix → fixed   stay → stayed
listen → listened   study → studied

Irregular verbs

buy → bought   have → had
drive → drove   meet → met
eat → ate   read → read
go → went   take → took

For additional irregular verbs, turn to page 152.

2 Practice

A Write. Complete the conversations. Use the simple past.

1. **A** What did Dahlia and her friends do on Sunday?

   B They ___*barbecued*___ hamburgers.
       (barbecue)

2. **A** What did the children do on Thursday?

   B They _____ a walk in the park.
       (take)

3. **A** What did your family do last weekend?

   B We _____ to the beach.
       (drive)

4. **A** What did Sarah do Monday night?

   B She _____ to the movies.
       (go)

5. **A** What did Nikos do Saturday morning?

   B He _____ the car.
       (fix)

6. **A** What did Carlos do Wednesday morning?

   B He _____ groceries.
       (buy)

Listen and repeat. Then practice with a partner.

B Talk with a partner. Change the **bold** words and make conversations.

> *A* What did **Alicia** do last weekend?
> *B* **She went shopping** and **read a book**.

1 Alicia

go shopping

read a book

2 John

eat in a restaurant

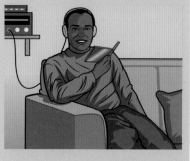

listen to music

3 Sam and Lisa

have a picnic

play soccer

C Talk with a partner. Change the **bold** words and make conversations. Look at the pictures in Exercise B.

> *A* Did **Alicia go shopping** last weekend?
> *B* **Yes, she did.**

> *A* Did **John play soccer** last weekend?
> *B* **No, he didn't. He listened to music.**

1. Alicia / go shopping
2. John / play soccer
3. Sam and Lisa / read a book
4. John / eat in a restaurant
5. Alicia / have a picnic
6. Sam and Lisa / play soccer

3 Communicate

Talk with your classmates. Ask and answer questions about last weekend.

> *A* Karen, did you go to the beach last weekend?
> *B* No, I didn't. I stayed home.

> *A* Marco, what did you do last weekend?
> *B* I studied for a test.

Lesson C — *When do you usually play soccer?*

1 Grammar focus: simple present vs. simple past

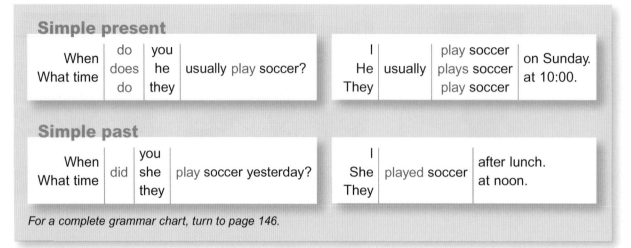

Simple present

When What time	do does do	you he they	usually play soccer?

	I He They	usually	play soccer plays soccer play soccer	on Sunday. at 10:00.

Simple past

When What time	did	you she they	play soccer yesterday?

	I She They	played soccer	after lunch. at noon.

For a complete grammar chart, turn to page 146.

2 Practice

A Write. Complete the conversations. Use the simple present or the simple past.

1. **A** When does Sharon usually meet her friends?

    B She usually ____meets____ her friends after work.

    A When did Sharon meet her friends yesterday?

    B Yesterday, she ____met____ them at noon for lunch.

2. **A** What time do Roberto and Selma usually eat dinner?

    B They usually _____ dinner at 7:00.

    A When did they eat dinner last night?

    B They _____ dinner at 8:00.

3. **A** When do Irma and Ron usually study?

    B They usually _____ on Saturday.

    A When did they study last weekend?

    B They _____ on Friday night.

4. **A** When do you usually watch movies?

    B I usually _____ movies after dinner.

    A What time did you watch a movie last night?

    B I _____ a movie at 6:00.

🔊 **Listen and repeat.** Then practice with a partner.

B Talk with a partner. Change the **bold** words and make conversations.

> **A** When does Karim usually **go to English class**?
> **B** He usually **goes to English class** at **8:00 a.m.**

1. 8:00 a.m. / go to English class
2. 11:30 a.m. / go to the gym
3. 2:00 p.m. / go to work
4. 9:00 p.m. / study

C Talk with a partner. Change the **bold** words and make conversations.

> **A** When did Maria **go shopping** last Saturday?
> **B** She **went shopping** at **10:00 a.m.**

1. 10:00 a.m. / go shopping
2. 1:00 p.m. / go to her citizenship class
3. 6:00 p.m. / clean her apartment
4. 7:30 p.m. / go to the movies

3 Communicate

Talk with your classmates. Ask and answer questions about daily activities.

> When do you usually get up?

> I usually get up at 7:00 a.m.

> When did you get up this morning?

> I got up at 7:30 a.m.

Lesson D Reading

1 Before you read

Look at the picture. Answer the questions.

1. Who is the woman?
2. What is she thinking about?

2 Read

SELF-STUDY
AUDIO CD

Read Rosa's journal. Listen and read again.

Thursday, June 20th

Today was a bad day! On Thursday, my children and I usually go to the park for a picnic, but today we had a problem. We drove to the store to buy groceries, and then the car broke down. I checked the engine, and there was a lot of smoke. Luckily, I had my cell phone! First, I called my husband at work. He left early, picked us up, and took us home. Next, I called the mechanic. Finally, I called Ling and asked for a ride to school tonight. In the end, we didn't go to the park because it was too late. Instead, we had a picnic in our backyard. Then, Ling drove me to school.

> Look for these words: *First, Next, Finally.*
> They tell the order of events.

3 After you read

A Write. Answer the questions about Rosa's day.

1. Where do Rosa and her children go on Thursday? *They go to the park.*
2. Why did they go to the store? _____
3. Who did Rosa call first? _____
4. Who picked up Rosa and the children? _____
5. What did Ling do? _____

B Number the sentences in the correct order.

_____ Ling drove Rosa to school.
_____ Rosa called her husband at work.
_____ Rosa's husband took them home.
_1_ Rosa went to the store.
_____ The car broke down.

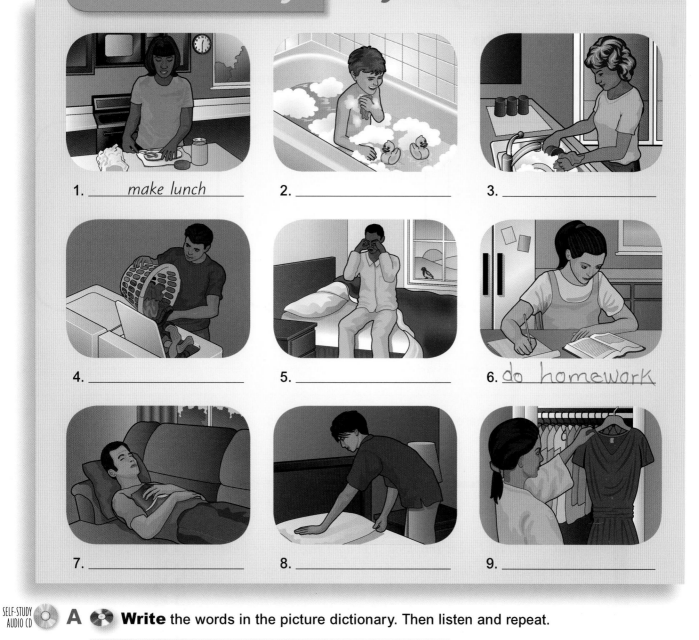

1. _make lunch_

2. _____

3. _____

4. _____

5. _____

6. do homework

7. _____

8. _____

9. _____

SELF-STUDY AUDIO CD

A 🔊 **Write** the words in the picture dictionary. Then listen and repeat.

do homework	get dressed	make the bed
do the dishes	get up	take a bath
do the laundry	make lunch	take a nap

B **Talk** with a partner. Change the **bold** words and make conversations.

A Did you **do the laundry** yesterday?
B Yes, I did.

A Did you **make the bed** this morning?
B No, I didn't. I **got up late**.

Writing

1 Before you write

A Write. Think about a day last week. Draw three pictures about that day. Write a sentence about each picture.

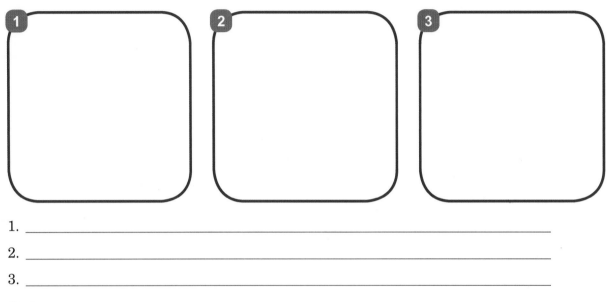

1. _____
2. _____
3. _____

Talk with a partner. Share your pictures and sentences.

B Read Tina's journal.

> Tuesday, September 1
>
> Last Saturday, I went shopping. I bought five bags of food. I put the groceries in the trunk of my car. Then, I drove home. When I got home, I didn't have my purse. It wasn't in the car, and it wasn't in the trunk. First, I drove back to the store. Next, I looked for my purse outside by the shopping carts, but I didn't find it. Finally, I went inside and asked the manager about my purse. He looked and found my purse in the Lost and Found. I was very happy. In the end, it was a good day.

Culture note
Many places have a *Lost and Found.* Go there to find lost things.

C Write. Answer the questions about Tina's day. Write complete sentences.

1. When did Tina go shopping? *She went shopping last Saturday.*
2. Where did she put the groceries? in the trunk of her car. trunk
3. Where did she first look for her purse? in the car and trunk
4. Where was her purse? in the Lost and Found

D Write. Read the sentences. Write *First, Next,* or *Finally* on the correct line.

1. Last Saturday, I did the laundry.

   _____ , I dried the clothes in the dryer.

   _____ , I folded the clean clothes.

   ___First___ , I washed the dirty clothes.

> Use a comma after sequence words.
> **First,** I washed the dirty clothes.

2. Last night, I stayed home.

   _____ , I washed the dishes.

   _____ , I cooked dinner.

   _____ , I went to bed.

3. Last Thursday, my family had a picnic.

   _____ , we ate breakfast.

   _____ , we woke up early.

   _____ , we went to the park.

E Write the sentences from Exercise D in the correct order.

1. *Last Saturday, I did the laundry. First, I washed the dirty clothes. Next,* _____

   _____

   _____

   _____

2. _____

   _____

   _____

   _____

3. _____

   _____

   _____

2 Write

Write a journal entry about a day in your life. Use Exercises 1A, 1B, and 1E to help you.

3 After you write

A Read your journal entry to a partner.

B Check your partner's journal entry.
- What kind of day did your partner have?
- What happened first?
- Are there commas after the sequence words (*First, Next, Finally*)?

Another view

1 Life-skills reading

E-Z Cell Phone
Calling Plans

Name	Cost	Monthly minutes	Additional minutes
Plan A	$59.00 a month	700	$0.45
Plan B	$79.00 a month	1,500	$0.30
Plan C	$149.00 a month	3,000	$0.20

A **Read** the questions. Look at the cell phone calling plans. Circle the answers.

1. Which plan costs $79.00 a month?
   a. Plan A
   b. Plan B
   c. Plan C
   d. E-Z Plan

2. How much is Plan C every month?
   a. $45.00
   b. $59.00
   c. $79.00
   d. $149.00

3. How much are additional minutes with Plan A?
   a. $0.20
   b. $0.30
   c. $0.45
   d. $0.59

4. How many monthly minutes come with Plan C?
   a. 149
   b. 700
   c. 1,500
   d. 3,000

B **Talk** with a partner. Ask and answer the questions.

1. Do you have a cell phone? If so, how long do you talk on it each day?
2. When do you usually call your friends? What do you talk about?
3. Sue usually talks on the phone about 15 hours a month. Which plan should she choose?

2 Fun with language

A **Work in a group.** Play a game. Write two true sentences about last week. Write one false sentence about last week.

I cooked dinner.
1.
2.
3.

Talk to your classmates. Read your three sentences out loud. Mix up the order. Your classmates guess which sentence is false.

> I think you didn't cook dinner.

B **Work in a group.** Ask questions about the past. Complete the chart.

> Pablo, did you go to a party last weekend?

> Yes, I did.

Find someone who:	
went to a party last weekend	*Pablo*
visited a friend last week	
called a friend last weekend	
had a party last year	
took a trip last summer	
played soccer last Saturday	
cooked breakfast yesterday	
went to the movies last month	
helped a friend yesterday	
got up late this morning	
did the dishes last night	

3 Wrap up

Complete the **Self-assessment** on page 142.

Get ready

1 Talk about the picture

A Look at the picture. What do you see?

B Point to a person who: has a headache • is holding an X-ray • hurt his leg
hurt her hand • is taking medicine • is on crutches

C Where are these people? What happened to them?

2 Listening

SELF-STUDY
AUDIO CD
A 🔘 **Listen.** Who is Hamid talking to? Write the letter of the conversation.

1. ____

2. ____

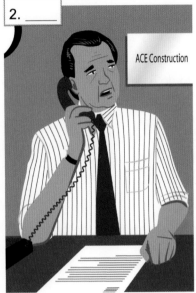

ACE Construction

3. ____

SELF-STUDY
AUDIO CD
B 🔘 **Listen again.** Write *T* (true) or *F* (false).

Conversation A

1. Hamid had an accident at home.   *F*

2. Hamid is at the hospital.   ____

3. Hamid will pick up his children.   ____

Conversation B

4. Hamid hurt his leg.   ____

5. Hamid had to get an X-ray.   ____

6. The hospital is on 53rd Street.   ____

Conversation C

7. Hamid works at Ace Construction.   ____

8. Hamid has to finish the paint job.   ____

9. Hamid will stay home tomorrow.   ____

Listen again. Check your answers.

C **Talk** with a partner. Ask and answer the questions.

1. What jobs are dangerous? Why?
2. Did you ever have an accident at work? What happened?
3. Did you ever have an accident at home? What happened?

Health   **45**

Lesson B *What do I have to do?*

1 Grammar focus: *have to* + verb

Questions					Answers		
What	do	I	have to do?		You	have to	
	does	he			He	has to	see a doctor.
	do	they			They	have to	

For a complete grammar chart, turn to page 147.

2 Practice

A Write. Complete the conversations. Use *have to* or *has to*, and *do* or *does*.

1. **A** Elian hurt his leg.

   What ___*does*___ he ___*have to*___ do?

   B He ___*has to*___ get an X-ray.

2. **A** Kathy and Tom have asthma.

   What _____ they _____ do?

   B They _____ take their medicine.

3. **A** My son broke his arm.

   What _____ I _____ do?

   B You _____ take him to the hospital.

4. **A** Marcia has a sprained ankle.

   What _____ she _____ do?

   B She _____ get a pair of crutches.

5. **A** Nick and Tony had an accident at work.

   What _____ they _____ do?

   B They _____ fill out an accident report.

6. **A** Pam hurt her back.

   What _____ she _____ do?

   B She _____ go home early.

   Listen and repeat. Then practice with a partner.

B Talk with a partner. Change the **bold** words and make conversations.

> **A** Here's your prescription. You have to **keep** this medicine **in the refrigerator**.
> **B** OK. I have to **keep** this medicine **in the refrigerator**.
> **A** Yes. Call me if you have any questions.

KEEP IN REFRIGERATOR
DO NOT FREEZE

TAKE IN THE MORNING

SHAKE WELL

TAKE WITH
FOOD

KEEP OUT OF REACH
OF CHILDREN

3 Communicate

Talk with a partner. What happened to these people? What do they have to do?

1

2

3

> She burned her hand.   She has to see a doctor.

Pharmex Original Copyrighted Warning Label information was printed with authorization from TimeMed Labeling Systems, Inc.

You should go to the hospital.

1 Grammar focus: *should*

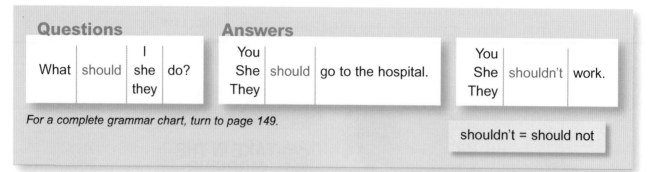

Questions				Answers						
What	should	I she they	do?	You She They	should	go to the hospital.		You She They	shouldn't	work.

For a complete grammar chart, turn to page 149.

shouldn't = should not

2 Practice

A Write. Complete the conversations.
Use *should* or *shouldn't*.

1. **A** Ken's eyes hurt. What _____*should*_____ he do?

   B He should rest. He ____*shouldn't*____ read right now.

2. **A** They have stomachaches. What _____ they do?

   B They _____ eat. They _____ take some medicine.

3. **A** My tooth hurts. What _____ I do?

   B You _____ see a dentist.

4. **A** Mia has a headache. What _____ she do?

   B She _____ take some aspirin.

5. **A** I hurt my leg. What _____ I do?

   B You _____ get an X-ray.

   You _____ walk.

6. **A** I have a bottle of medicine.

   What _____ I do?

   B You _____ keep it in the refrigerator.

   You _____ freeze it.

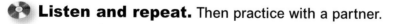 **Listen and repeat.** Then practice with a partner.

B Look at the pictures. Al is gardening. It's very hot. Check (✓) the things he should do.

☐ Drink lots of water.

☐ Wear heavy clothes.

☐ Take a break.

☐ Use a wet towel.

☐ Stay in the sun.

☐ Stay in the shade.

Talk with a partner. Look at the pictures again. Change the **bold** words and make conversations.

> **A** Al doesn't feel well. What should he do?
> **B** He should **drink lots of water**. He shouldn't **stay in the sun**.
> **A** OK. I'll tell him.

Useful language
I'll tell him.
I'll let him know.

3 Communicate

Talk in a group. Read the problems. Give advice.

Teresa's wrist is very sore. What should she do?

Ed is very hot. He doesn't feel well. What should he do?

Susana fell off her chair. What should her mother do?

Lesson D Reading

1 Before you read

Look at the picture. Answer the questions.

1. Who is the man?
2. What is he doing?
3. What should he do?

2 Read

SELF-STUDY AUDIO CD

Read the warning label. Listen and read again.

WARNING:
PREVENT ACCIDENTS.
READ BEFORE USING!

- Face the ladder when climbing up and down.
- Don't carry a lot of equipment while climbing a ladder – wear a tool belt.
- Never stand on the shelf of the ladder – stand on the steps.
- Never stand on the top step of a ladder.
- Be safe! Always read and follow the safety stickers.

Lists often begin with a number or bullet (•). Each numbered or bulleted item is a new idea.

3 After you read

A Write. Complete the sentences. Use *should* or *shouldn't*.

1. You _____shouldn't_____ carry a lot of equipment while climbing a ladder.
2. You _____ read and follow the safety stickers.
3. You _____ face the ladder when climbing up or down.
4. You _____ stand on the shelf of the ladder.

B Write. Complete the paragraph.

| accidents | ladder | safe | safety | tool belt |

> **Culture note**
> In emergencies, dial 911 for help.

Be Careful in the Workplace!

Don't have _____accidents_____ at work. Always read the _____
                     1   2
stickers on your tools and equipment. When you climb a _____ , wear
                                                              3
a _____ . When you carry heavy items, ask someone to help you.
        4
We want our workers to be _____ and healthy.
                                    5

50   Unit 4

Picture dictionary   Health problems

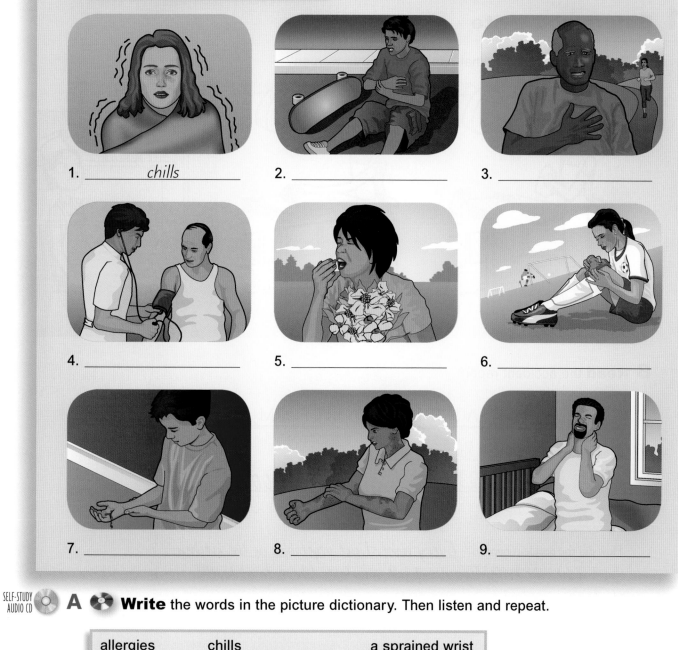

1. _chills_

2. _____

3. _____

4. _____

5. _____

6. _____

7. _____

8. _____

9. _____

SELF-STUDY
AUDIO CD

A **Write** the words in the picture dictionary. Then listen and repeat.

allergies	chills	a sprained wrist
a bad cut	high blood pressure	a stiff neck
chest pains	a rash	a swollen knee

B **Talk** with a partner. Change the **bold** words and make conversations.

A **She** has **chills**. What should **she** do?
B **She** should **stay in bed and rest**.

1 Before you write

A Talk with a partner. What happened to this woman?

B Read the accident report.

ACCIDENT REPORT FORM

Employee name: *Komiko Yanaka*

Date of accident: *January 13, 2008*   Time: *9:00 p.m.*

Type of injury: *cut foot*

How did the accident happen? *Every night, I cut vegetables in the kitchen. Last night, the knife slipped and cut my foot. I have to go to the doctor tomorrow.*

Signature: *Komiko Yanaka*   Date: *1/14/08*

C Write. Answer the questions about the accident report.

1. Who had an accident? *Komiko Yanaka.*
2. When did the accident happen? _____
3. What was the injury? _____
4. How did the injury happen? _____
5. When did she complete the form? _____

D Write. Work with a partner. Read the sentences. Number the sentences in the correct order.

1. Yesterday, I cut my foot.
   ____ It fell on my foot.
   ____ The knife slipped.
   _1_ I was in the kitchen.

2. Yesterday, I sprained my ankle.
   ____ There was water on the floor.
   ____ I have to fill out an accident report.
   ____ I slipped.

3. Yesterday, I broke my leg.
   ____ I fell.
   ____ I went to the hospital.
   ____ I was at the top of a ladder.

4. Yesterday, I hurt my back.
   ____ I felt a terrible pain in my back.
   ____ I picked up a heavy box.
   ____ I have to see a doctor tomorrow.

2 Write

Complete the accident report form. Use your imagination or write about a real accident. Use Exercises 1B and 1D to help you.

ACCIDENT REPORT FORM

Employee name: _____

Date of accident: _____   Time: _____

Type of injury: _____

How did the accident happen? _____

_____

_____

_____

_____

Signature: _____ Date: _____

---

3 After you write

A Read your form to a partner.

B Check your partner's form.
- What was the injury?
- What was the date of the accident?
- Is there a signature on the form?

Your signature on a form makes it official.
For a signature, use cursive writing.
Don't print.

Carl Staley
~~Carl Staley~~

Another view

1 Life-skills reading

Drug facts	
Active ingredient (in each tablet)	**Purpose**
Acetaminophen 325 mg	Pain reliever
Uses Temporary relief of minor aches and pains	
Warnings	
Ask a doctor or pharmacist before use if you are taking a prescription drug.	
Ask a doctor before use if you have liver or kidney disease.	
When using this product, do not take more than directed.	
Can cause drowsiness.	
Keep out of reach of children.	
Directions	
Adults and children 12 years and over: Take 2 tablets every 4 to 6 hours as needed. Do not take more than 8 tablets in 24 hours.	
Children under 12 years of age: Ask a doctor.	

A **Read** the questions. Look at the medicine label. Circle the answers.

1. Why should you take this medicine?
   a. for aches and pains
   b. for drowsiness
   c. for kidney disease
   d. for liver disease

2. How many tablets should children under 12 take at one time?
   a. 2 tablets
   b. 4 tablets
   c. no tablets
   d. none of the above

3. How many tablets should an adult take at one time?
   a. 2 tablets
   b. 4 tablets
   c. 6 tablets
   d. 8 tablets

4. How many tablets can an adult take in one day?
   a. 8 tablets
   b. 12 tablets
   c. 24 tablets
   d. none of the above

B **Talk** with a partner. Ask and answer the questions.

1. Your father has a headache. How many tablets should you give him?
2. Your son is four years old. Should you give him any tablets?
3. Jane has kidney disease. She wants to take a tablet. What does she have to do first?
4. Paul is taking a prescription drug. He wants to take this medicine. What should he do?

2 Fun with language

A Work with a partner. Complete the sentences.

accident	blood pressure	hurt	medicine
aspirin	fell off	label	

1. Be careful. Those boxes are heavy. Don't (h) u r t your back.

2. Rosa needs to see a doctor. She has high ___ ___ ___ ___ ___
   ◯___ ___ ___ ◯___ ___ ___ .

3. I have asthma. I have to take ___ ___ ___ ◯ ___ ___ ___ .

4. Always read the warning ___ ___ ___ ___ ◯ .

5. He has a headache. He should take some ◯ ___ ___ ___ ___ ___ .

6. Ray ___ ___ ___ ___ ◯ ___ ___ the ladder.

7. Todd sprained his ankle at work. He has to fill out an
   ___ ___ ___ ___ ___ ___ ___ ◯ report.

Write the circled letters from the sentences.

   h ___ ___ ___ ___ ___ ___

Write. Unscramble the letters to answer the question.

Where should you go if you are hurt?

   h ___ ___ ___ ___ ___ ___ ___

B Work in a group. Look at the sayings. What do they mean?

1. Laughter is the best medicine.
2. An apple a day keeps the doctor away.
3. Health is better than wealth.

Share your answers with another group.

3 Wrap up

Complete the **Self-assessment** on page 142.

Review

1 Listening

🔵 **Read** the questions. Then listen and circle the answers.

1. What does Trinh do?
   (a.) She's a nurse.
   b. She's a waitress.

2. Where does she work?
   a. at a hospital
   b. at a restaurant

3. Who became citizens last weekend?
   a. Trinh and her husband
   b. Trinh and her family

4. What did Trinh and her husband do at the beach?
   a. They took pictures.
   b. They took a nap.

5. When did they have a barbecue?
   a. in the afternoon
   b. in the evening

6. What did they do at home?
   a. They watched a movie.
   b. They read.

Talk with a partner. Ask and answer the questions. Use complete sentences.

2 Grammar

A **Write.** Complete the story.

At the Doctor's Office

Yesterday, Manuel's wife, Serena, _____*took*_____ him to Dr. Scott's

1. take

office. Dr. Scott _____ Manuel that he _____ weight.

2. tell   3. should / lose

Manuel usually _____ a lot of fried food. He _____ a

4. eat   5. drink

lot of coffee and soda. Dr. Scott said Manuel _____ more fruit and

6. should / eat

vegetables and drink more water. She said that Manuel _____ .

7. should / exercise

Now he _____ walk every day.

8. have to

B **Write.** Look at the answers. Write the questions.

1. **A** Where _did Serena take Manuel_ ?
   B Serena took Manuel to Dr. Scott's office.

2. **A** What _____ ?
   B He usually eats fried food.

3. **A** What _____ ?
   B He should eat fruit and vegetables.

4. **A** What _____ ?
   B He has to exercise.

Talk with a partner. Ask and answer the questions.

3 Pronunciation: important words

A 🔊 **Listen** to the important words in these sentences.

Tina's **car** broke down.
Oscar has to take his **medicine**.

B 🔊 **Listen and repeat.** Clap for each word. Clap loudly for the important word.

1. His **wife** had to do it.
2. Van has a **headache**.
3. I played **soccer** last night.
4. They went to the **library** yesterday.
5. Eliza **works** in the afternoon.
6. **Sam** made breakfast.

C 🔊 **Listen** for the important word in each sentence. Underline the important word.

1. Ali cut his <u>arm</u>.
2. He went to the hospital.
3. His sister took him.
4. He saw the doctor.
5. He has to take some medicine.
6. He shouldn't carry heavy items.

Talk with a partner. Compare your answers.

D Write four sentences from Units 3 and 4. Then work with a partner. Underline the important words in your partner's sentences.

1.
2.
3.
4.

Talk with a partner. Read the sentences.

Get ready

1 Talk about the picture

A Look at the picture. What do you see?

B Point to: an information desk • a departure board • a track number
a ticket booth • a suitcase • a waiting area

C Where are these people? What are they doing?

2 Listening

A **Listen.** What is Binh talking about? Write the letter of the conversation.

1. ____

2. ____

3. ____

B **Listen again.** Write *T* (true) or *F* (false).

Conversation A

1. Trains for Washington, D.C., leave every hour.   *T*

2. The next train to Washington, D.C., will leave at 8:00.   ____

3. The next train to Washington, D.C., will leave from Track 1.   ____

Conversation B

4. Trains to New York leave every hour.   ____

5. The next train to New York will leave at 7:35.   ____

6. Binh and his mother need to buy tickets.   ____

Conversation C

7. Binh never travels by train.   ____

8. It takes about two hours to drive to New York.   ____

9. It takes two and a half hours to get to New York by train.   ____

Listen again. Check your answers.

C **Talk** with a partner. How do you get to work? How do you get to school?

> I go to work by bus, and I walk to school.

> I take the train to work, and I drive to school.

How often? How long?

1 Grammar focus: *How often?* and *How long?*

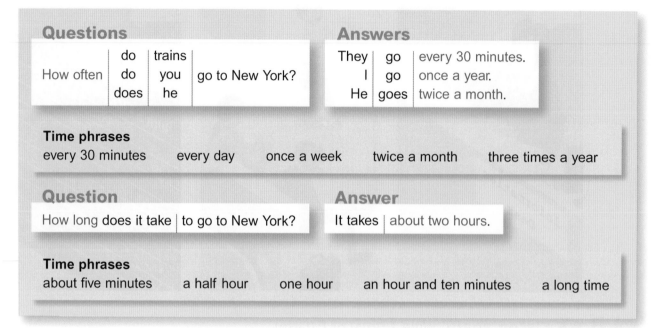

Questions

How often	do do does	trains you he	go to New York?

Answers

They I He	go go goes	every 30 minutes. once a year. twice a month.

Time phrases

every 30 minutes   every day   once a week   twice a month   three times a year

Question

How long does it take	to go to New York?

Answer

It takes	about two hours.

Time phrases

about five minutes   a half hour   one hour   an hour and ten minutes   a long time

2 Practice

A Write. Circle the correct answers.

1. *A* How often does Binh go to New York?
   B 30 minutes. / (Twice a month.)

2. *A* How long does it take to fly to Mexico?
   B A long time. / Once a month.

3. *A* How often do you study?
   B Three hours. / Twice a week.

4. *A* How long does it take to drive to Toronto?
   B Seven hours. / Once a day.

5. *A* How long does it take to walk to school?
   B Twice a week. / 20 minutes.

6. *A* How often does Sandra cook dinner?
   B Two hours. / Three times a week.

7. *A* How often does the bus go to Springfield?
   B Once a day. / A long time.

8. *A* How often do they go on vacation?
   B A long time. / Once a year.

9. *A* How long does it take to drive to the airport?
   B One hour. / Twice a year.

10. *A* How long does it take to walk to the library?
    B Every 30 minutes. / 25 minutes.

Listen and repeat. Then practice with a partner.

B Read the bus schedule. Where does the bus go?

Springfield to New York City			Springfield to Capital Airport		
Departs	Arrives	Duration	Departs	Arrives	Duration
6:30 a.m.	9:00 a.m.	2h 30m	5:30 a.m.	6:50 a.m.	1h 20m
11:00 a.m.	1:30 p.m.	2h 30m	9:00 a.m.	10:20 a.m.	1h 20m
2:00 p.m.	4:30 p.m.	2h 30m	3:00 p.m.	4:20 p.m.	1h 20m
6:30 p.m.	9:00 p.m.	2h 30m	5:00 p.m.	6:20 p.m.	1h 20m
			6:00 p.m.	7:20 p.m.	1h 20m

Springfield to Boston			Springfield to Washington, D.C.		
Departs	Arrives	Duration	Departs	Arrives	Duration
8:00 a.m.	4:15 p.m.	8h 15m	7:45 a.m.	11:15 a.m.	3h 30m
9:30 a.m.	5:45 p.m.	8h 15m	9:45 a.m.	1:15 p.m.	3h 30m
11:00 a.m.	7:15 p.m.	8h 15m	11:00 a.m.	2:30 p.m.	3h 30m
			1:00 p.m.	4:30 p.m.	3h 30m

USBus

Schedule

h = hour   m = minute

C Talk with a partner. Change the **bold** words and make conversations.

A Excuse me. How often do buses go to **New York City**?
B They go **four** times a day.
A How long does it take to get there?
B It takes about **two and a half hours**.

Useful language
two and a half hours = two hours and 30 minutes
a half hour = half an hour = 30 minutes

1. New York City   2. Boston   3. Washington, D.C.   4. the airport

3 Communicate

Talk with a partner. Ask questions. Complete the chart.

A How often do you walk to school?
B I walk to school every day. OR
I don't walk to school. I take a bus.

A How long does it take?
B It takes about half an hour.

	How often?	How long?
walk to school	*every day*	*half an hour*
take the bus to work		
drive to the store		
fly to another country		

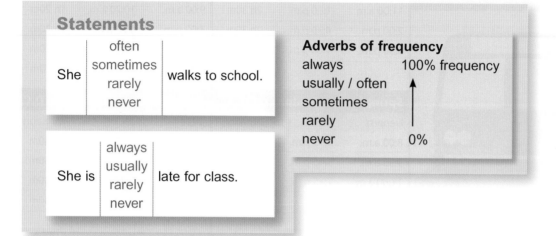

Lesson C *She often walks to school.*

1 Grammar focus: adverbs of frequency

Statements

| She | often
sometimes
rarely
never | walks to school. |

| She is | always
usually
rarely
never | late for class. |

Adverbs of frequency

always	100% frequency
usually / often	
sometimes	
rarely	
never	0%

2 Practice

A **Write.** Use adverbs of frequency and make new sentences.

1. Teresa drives to work in the morning.
   Teresa always drives to work in the morning.
   (always)

2. She is late.
   _____
   (rarely)

3. Her husband walks to work.
   _____
   (usually)

4. He takes a taxi.
   _____
   (sometimes)

5. He drives.
   _____
   (never)

6. Their daughter rides her bike to school.
   _____
   (always)

7. She is tired in the morning.
   _____
   (often)

Listen and repeat. Check your answers.

B **Talk** with a partner. Change the **bold** words and make conversations.

John		Never	Rarely	Usually	Always
	1. walks to school	✓			
	2. drives to school				✓
	3. is tired in the morning		✓		
	4. is hungry around 11:00			✓	

Sunita		Never	Sometimes	Often	Always
	1. walks to school			✓	
	2. drives to school		✓		
	3. is tired in the morning				✓
	4. is hungry around 11:00	✓			

A John **never walks to school**.
How about Sunita?
B She **often walks to school**.

Useful language
How about . . . ?
What about . . . ?

3 Communicate

A **Write.** Complete the sentences about yourself.

1. I usually ___eat lunch___ after class.
2. I am often _____ on Saturday.
3. I usually _____ during the summer.
4. I am never _____ in the afternoon.
5. I sometimes _____ late at night.
6. I always _____ on the weekend.
7. I rarely _____ in the morning.
8. I never _____ during the week.

B **Talk** with a partner. Use your answers from Exercise A.

I usually eat lunch after class. What about you?

I usually go to work.

1 Before you read

Look at the picture. Answer the questions.

1. Who do you see in the picture?
2. Where is she?
3. What is she doing?

2 Read

SELF-STUDY
AUDIO CD

Read the letter. Listen and read again.

Dear Layla,

Right now, my mother is visiting me here in Philadelphia. I rarely see her because she comes to Philadelphia only once a year. She usually stays for one month. Here is a photo of my mother at the airport last week. She was happy to see me!

This year, I want to take my mother to New York City. I want to show her the Statue of Liberty and Central Park. It takes about one and a half hours to get to New York by train. We are excited about our trip. Can you meet us there? Let me know.

Your friend,
Binh

> Capital letters can show you the names of cities or places.
> **N**ew **Y**ork **C**ity
> **S**tatue of **L**iberty

3 After you read

Write. Correct the sentences.

1. Binh's mother comes to Philadelphia three times a year.
   Binh's mother comes to Philadelphia once a year.

2. Binh often sees his mother.
   _____

3. Binh wants to take his mother to Los Angeles.
   _____

4. Binh wants to show his mother the White House.
   _____

5. It takes two hours to get from Philadelphia to New York by train.
   _____

1. _go shopping_

2. _____

3. _____

4. _____

5. _____

6. _____

7. _____

8. _____

9. _____

SELF-STUDY
AUDIO CD

A **Write** the words in the picture dictionary. Then listen and repeat.

buy souvenirs	go swimming	take a suitcase
go shopping	stay at a hotel	take pictures
go sightseeing	stay with relatives	write postcards

B **Talk** with a partner. Change the **bold** words and make conversations.

A Do you **go shopping** on a trip?
B Yes, I do. I always **go shopping**.

A Do you **stay at a hotel** on a trip?
B No, I don't. I never **stay at a hotel**.

1 Before you write

A Talk with a partner. Ask and answer the questions.

1. When was your last trip?
2. Where did you go?
3. What did you do there?

B Read the letter from Alicia.

> Dear Margarita,
>   How are you? I just got back from a trip to California. I went to visit my cousin, Isaac. Isaac lives in San Diego. I always go to visit him once a year. It usually takes about six hours to get there from Boston by plane.
>   This year we drove to San Francisco for three days. We went sightseeing. I saw the Golden Gate Bridge and Pier 39. We also went shopping, and I bought souvenirs. It was a fun trip!
>   Hope you are well. Write soon!
>
>   Your friend,
>   Alicia

C Write. Answer the questions about Alicia's letter. Write complete sentences.

1. Where did Alicia go? _Alicia went to California._
2. Who did she visit? _____
3. How often does she go there? _____
4. How long does it usually take to get there? _____
   _____
5. What did she do there? _____
   _____
   _____

D Write. Answer the questions about yourself.

1. When was your last trip?

   _____

   _____

2. Where did you go?

   _____

   _____

3. How did you get there?

   _____

   _____

4. How often do you go there?

   _____

   _____

5. How long does it usually take to get there?

   _____

   _____

6. Who did you go with?

   _____

   _____

7. What did you do there?

   _____

   _____

   _____

> **Useful language**
> *How did you get there?*
> *By train.*   *By bus.*
> *By plane.*   *By car.*

2 Write

Write a letter to a friend about your last trip.
Use Exercises 1B and 1D to help you.

> Spell out hours and minutes from one to ten:
> **one** hour and **five** minutes
>
> Write all other time numbers:
> **11** hours and **30** minutes

3 After you write

A Read your letter to a partner.

B Check your partner's letter.

- Where did your partner go?
- How long does it usually take to get there?
- Did your partner write the hours and minutes correctly?

Lesson F *Another view*

1 Life-skills reading

MetroTrack Train Schedule

Train	From	To	Departs	Arrives
763 EXPRESS	PHILADELPHIA	NEW YORK	6:35 A.M.	7:35 A.M.
565	PHILADELPHIA	NEW YORK	6:55 A.M.	8:05 A.M.
567	PHILADELPHIA	NEW YORK	7:25 A.M.	8:44 A.M.
769 EXPRESS	PHILADELPHIA	NEW YORK	7:50 A.M.	8:50 A.M.
573	PHILADELPHIA	NEW YORK	8:22 A.M.	9:40 A.M.
775	PHILADELPHIA	NEW YORK	8:43 A.M.	10:00 A.M.
583	PHILADELPHIA	NEW YORK	10:47 A.M.	12:00 NOON

A Read the questions. Look at the train schedule. Circle the answers.

1. How long does it take to go to New York on Train 763?
   a. one hour
   b. one hour and five minutes
   c. one hour and ten minutes
   d. one hour and 15 minutes

2. How often does the express train go to New York before 11:00 a.m.?
   a. once
   b. twice
   c. three times
   d. eight times

3. How long does it take to go to New York on Train 565?
   a. one hour and five minutes
   b. one hour and ten minutes
   c. an hour and a half
   d. two hours and ten minutes

4. How many trains arrive in New York before 9:00 a.m.?
   a. one train
   b. two trains
   c. three trains
   d. four trains

B Talk with a partner. Ask and answer the questions.

1. How long does it take to go from Philadelphia to New York on Train 769?
2. How many trains go from Philadelphia to New York in the morning?
3. What time does the first train leave Philadelphia to go to New York?
4. What time does the last train leave Philadelphia to go to New York?

68   Unit 5

2 Fun with language

A Write. Complete the chart with your own information. Check (✓) the answers.

How often do you	Always	Often / Usually	Sometimes	Rarely	Never
stay at a hotel?					
stay with relatives?					
fly on a plane?					
go sightseeing?					
take pictures?					
write postcards?					
go on vacation?					
take a trip?					

Work with a partner. Talk about your charts.

> I often stay with relatives. I stay with relatives five or six times a year.

> I rarely stay with relatives. I stay with relatives only once or twice a year.

B Work in a group. Ask questions.

> Danny, how often do you drive a truck?

> Almost every day.

Find someone who:	
usually drives a truck	*Danny*
often takes a bus	
never takes a train	
rarely walks	
sometimes rides a bike	
always drives a car	

3 Wrap up

Complete the **Self-assessment** on page 143.

Lesson A *Get ready*

1 Talk about the picture

A Look at the picture. What do you see?

B Point to: a class picture • a family picture • a photo album
        a baby picture • a graduation picture • a wedding picture

C Look at the people. What are they doing?

Olga

Victoria

2 Listening

  A  **Listen.** What is Olga talking about? Write the letter of the conversation.

1. _____

2. _____

3. _____

  B  **Listen again.** Write *T* (true) or *F* (false).

Conversation A

1. Olga moved into her apartment two months ago.   *T*

2. Olga got married in 1993.   _____

3. Victoria got married 30 years ago.   _____

Conversation B

4. Sergey is 14.   _____

5. Sergey started college in September.   _____

6. Natalya started college on Tuesday.   _____

Conversation C

7. Olga met her husband in Moscow.   _____

8. Olga moved to Russia about 14 years ago.   _____

9. Natalya was born in Russia.   _____

Listen again. Check your answers.

C Talk with a partner. Ask and answer the questions.

1. When do children start high school and college in countries you know?
2. At what age do people get married in countries you know?
3. When do people usually start their first jobs?

When did you move here?

1 Grammar focus: *When* questions and simple past

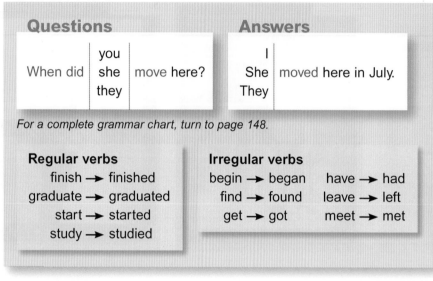

Questions			Answers	
When did	you she they	move here?	I She They	moved here in July.

For a complete grammar chart, turn to page 148.

Regular verbs
finish → finished
graduate → graduated
start → started
study → studied

Irregular verbs
begin → began   have → had
find → found   leave → left
get → got   meet → met

2 Practice

A Write. Complete the conversations. Use the simple past.

1. **A** When did Min leave Korea?
   B She ___left___ Korea in 1974.
   A When did she move to New York?
   B She _____ to New York in 1995.

2. **A** When did Carlos start school?
   B He _____ school in September.
   A When did he graduate?
   B He _____ in June.

3. **A** When did Paul and Amy meet?
   B They _____ in 2003.
   A When did they get married?
   B They _____ married in 2005.

Listen and repeat. Then practice with a partner.

B **Read** Kasem's and Kanya's time lines.

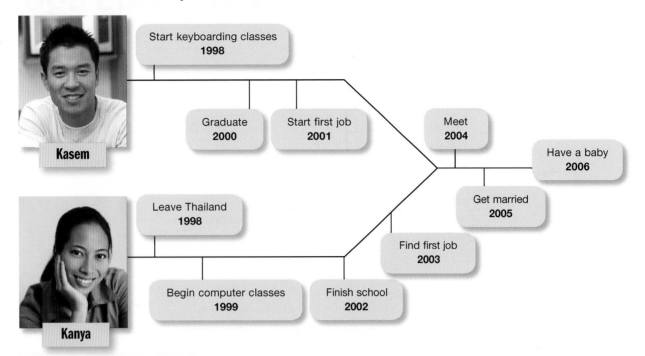

Kasem

Start keyboarding classes
1998

Graduate
2000

Start first job
2001

Meet
2004

Have a baby
2006

Get married
2005

Find first job
2003

Kanya

Leave Thailand
1998

Begin computer classes
1999

Finish school
2002

Talk with a partner. Change the **bold** words and make conversations.

> **A** When did **Kasem start keyboarding classes**?
> **B** **He started keyboarding classes** in **1998**.

1. Kasem / start keyboarding classes
2. Kanya / begin computer classes
3. Kasem / graduate
4. Kasem and Kanya / meet
5. Kanya / find her first job
6. Kasem and Kanya / have a baby
7. Kanya / finish school
8. Kasem and Kanya / get married
9. Kanya / leave Thailand
10. Kasem / start his first job

3 Communicate

Talk with a partner. Complete the chart.

> **A** Ali, when did you start English classes?
> **B** I started English classes in 2006.

Useful language
I was born here.

start English classes	*in 2006*
move to this country	
start your first job	

He graduated two years ago.

1 Grammar focus: time phrases

Statements

He graduated	two years ago. two weeks ago. in May. in 2004. on Wednesday. on May 4th, 2004.	She got married	at 3:00 p.m. at 12:00 noon. before she came to the U.S. after she came to the U.S. last year. this week.

2 Practice

A Write. Complete the conversations. Use *at*, *in*, *on*, or *ago*.

1. **A** When did Lou and Angela buy their new car?

   B They bought their new car _three weeks ago_ .
   (three weeks)

2. **A** When did Lou and Angela get married?

   B They got married _Four years ago_
   (four years)

3. **A** When did Angela have a baby?

   B She had a baby yesterday _at 8:20 a.m._
   (8:20 a.m.)

4. **A** When did Lou begin his new job?

   B He began his new job _on Tuesday_ .
   (Tuesday)

5. **A** When did Lou move to the United States?

   B He moved to the United States _on December 15th_
   (December 15th)

6. **A** When did Angela come to the United States?

   B She came to the United States _three years ago_
   (three years)

7. **A** When did Angela take the citizenship exam?

   B She took the citizenship exam _in March_ .
   (March)

   Listen and repeat. Then practice with a partner.

> **Culture note**
> The citizenship exam is a test you have to take to become an American citizen.

B **Write.** Complete the sentences. Use *at*, *in*, or *on*.

1

Anna graduated
_in_ 1998.

2

She got married
_on_ Saturday,
August 16th, 2001.

3

She had a baby _on_
June 21st, 2003,
_at_ 2:30 a.m.

4

She and her family
moved to the United
States _in_ 2005.

5

She bought a house
_in_ April.

6

She took the
citizenship exam
_on_ May 16th.

7

She became a citizen
_on_ Tuesday.

8

She started her new
job yesterday _at_
9:00 a.m.

Talk with a partner. Change the **bold** words and make conversations.
Use *before* or *after*.

> **A** When did Anna **graduate**?
> **B** She **graduated before** she
> moved to the United States.

1. graduate
2. buy a house
3. become a citizen

4. get married
5. take the citizenship exam
6. have a baby

3 Communicate

Read. What did you do? Check (✓) the boxes.

- ☑ get married
- ☑ have a baby
- ☐ get a driver's license
- ☑ get a new job

- ☐ register for English class
- ☐ buy a car
- ☑ move here
- ☐ study computers

Useful language
I'm not married.
I don't have children.
I didn't study computers.

Talk with a partner. Ask and answer questions.

> **A** When did you get married?
> **B** I got married three years ago on August 25th.

Lesson D Reading

1 Before you read

Look at the picture. Answer the questions.

1. Who are the people?
2. Where are they?
3. What are they doing?

2 Read

SELF-STUDY
AUDIO CD

Read the interview. Listen and read again.

An Interesting Life

Interviewer:	What happened after you graduated from high school?
Olga:	I went to university in Moscow, and I met my husband there. It was a long time ago! We were in the same class. We fell in love and got married on April 2nd, 1983. We had a small wedding in Moscow.
Interviewer:	What happened after you got married?
Olga:	I finished university and found a job. I was a teacher. Then, I had a baby. My husband and I were very excited to have a little boy.
Interviewer:	When did you move to the United States?
Olga:	We immigrated about 14 years ago. We became American citizens ten years ago.

The interviewer's questions tell you what the interview is about.

3 After you read

A Write. Answer the questions about Olga.

1. When did Olga meet her husband? _A long time ago._
2. When did they get married? _____
3. When did they become American citizens? _____
4. When did she and her family move to the U.S.? _____

B Number the sentences in the correct order.

____ Olga had a baby boy.   ____ She met her husband.

____ She moved to the U.S.   ____ She became a U.S. citizen.

____ She found a job.   _1_ Olga graduated from high school.

____ Olga got married.   ____ Olga finished university.

76   Unit 6

4 Picture dictionary — Life events

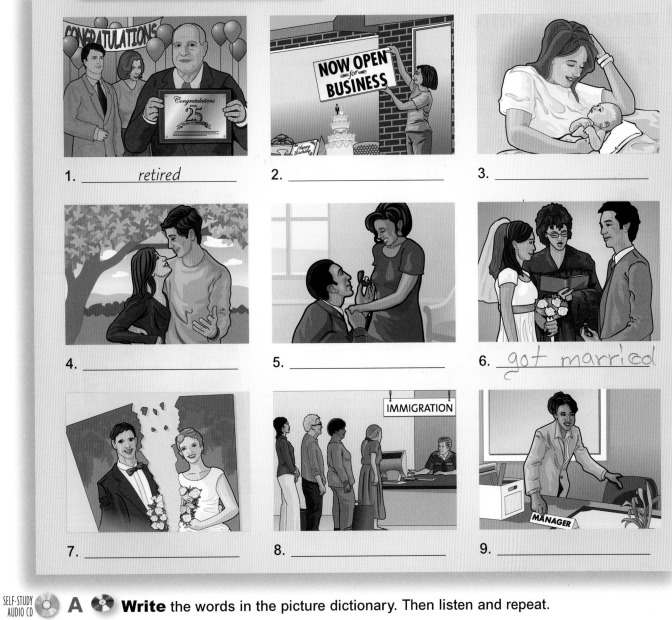

1. _retired_
2. _____
3. _____

4. _____
5. _____
6. _got married_

7. _____
8. _____
9. _____

A **Write** the words in the picture dictionary. Then listen and repeat.

fell in love	got married	immigrated
got a divorce	got promoted	retired
got engaged	had a baby	started a business

B **Talk** with a partner. Which life events happened to you? When did they happen? What happened after that?

> I retired two years ago. After I retired, I started English classes.

Lesson E *Writing*

1 Before you write

A Talk with a partner. Ask and answer the questions.

1. What three events were important in your life?
2. When was each event?

Write. Make a time line. Use your partner's information.

My partner's time line

1. _____
2. _____
3. _____

B Read about Bo-Hai in his company newsletter.

■ **COMPUTER** SYSTEMS INC.

■ **A New Employee: Bo-Hai Cheng**

I was born in 1983 in Beijing. I started university in 2001. I studied civil engineering. In 2004, I moved to Miami. After I moved, I bought a car. I also got engaged. Then I studied computers at a vocational school. I graduated on July 3rd. Three weeks ago, I found a computer job. In October, I'm going to get married!

C Write. Complete Bo-Hai's time line.

bought a car	graduated from vocational school	started university
found a job	moved to Miami	was born in 1983

Bo-Hai's time line

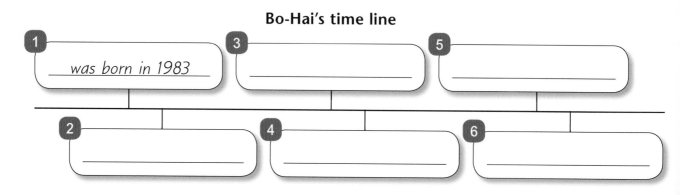

1. *was born in 1983*
2. _____
3. _____
4. _____
5. _____
6. _____

D **Write** each sentence a different way.

1. I started college in 2001.

   In 2001, I started college.

2. In 2004, I moved to Miami.

   _____

3. I graduated on July 3rd.

   _____

4. Three weeks ago, I found a computer job.

   _____

5. In October, I'm going to get married.

   _____

> Use a comma (,) after time phrases like *In 2001* or *On July 3rd* at the beginning of a sentence.

E **Write.** Complete the time line about yourself.

My time line

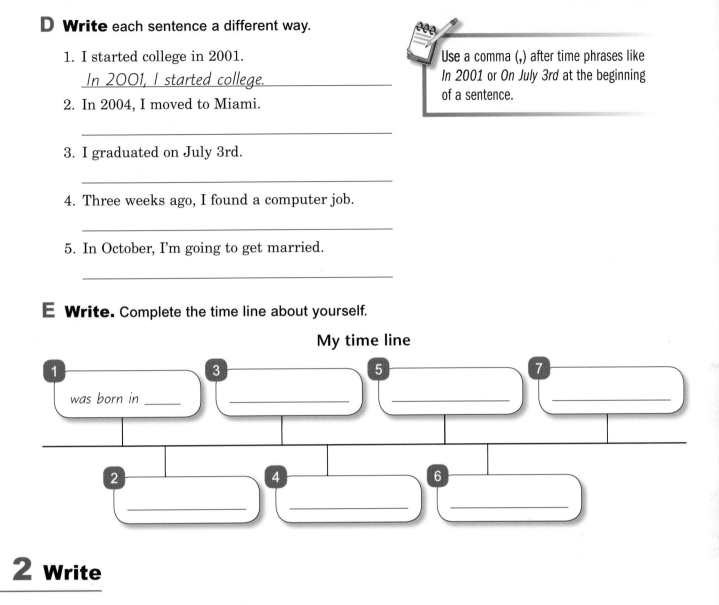

1 *was born in* _____

2 _____

3 _____

4 _____

5 _____

6 _____

7 _____

2 Write

Write a paragraph about yourself. Use Exercises 1B and 1E to help you.

3 After you write

A **Read** your paragraph to a partner.

B **Check** your partner's paragraph.

- What are the important events?
- What time phrases are in the paragraph?
- Are there commas after time phrases at the beginning of sentences?

Another view

1 Life-skills reading

APPLICATION FOR A MARRIAGE LICENSE

Groom's Personal Data

1A. Name of Groom (First)	1B. Middle	1C. Last	2. Birthdate (Mo / Day / Yr)
Antonio	Marco	Velez	06/12/83

3A. Residence (Street & Number)	3B. City	3C. Zip Code	3D. State	4. Place of Birth
16 Ocean Parkway, Apt. 6A	San Diego	92124	CA	Mexico City, Mexico

5. Number of Previous Marriages	6A. Last Marriage Ended by	6B. Date (Mo / Day / Yr)
1	Divorce	08/13/07

Bride's Personal Data

1A. Name of Bride (First)	1B. Middle	1C. Last	2. Birthdate (Mo / Day / Yr)
Maria	Luisa	Camacho	11/17/87

3A. Residence (Street & Number)	3B. City	3C. Zip Code	3D. State	4. Place of Birth
1994 Grant Avenue, Apt. 403	San Diego	92124	CA	Lima, Peru

5. Number of Previous Marriages	6A. Last Marriage Ended by	6B. Date (Mo / Day / Yr)
None		

Groom's Driver's License / I.D.#:	Bride's Driver's License / I.D.#:
CO581316429	CO901516531

Ceremony Date:	Ceremony Location:
June 20, 2009	City Hall

A Read the questions. Look at the application for a marriage license. Circle the answers.

1. When was the bride born?
   a. in 1985
   b. in 1987
   c. in 1994
   d. in 2007

2. When was the groom born?
   a. on June 12, 1983
   b. on December 6, 1983
   c. on August 13, 1984
   d. on November 17, 1987

3. When did the groom get divorced?
   a. in 1997
   b. in 2001
   c. in 2007
   d. in 2010

4. When is their wedding ceremony?
   a. on 6/2/08
   b. on 2/6/09
   c. on 6/20/09
   d. on 6/28/09

B Talk with a partner. Ask and answer the questions.

1. When was the last wedding you attended?
2. Where was the ceremony?
3. Who were the bride and groom? Where did they meet?

2 Fun with language

Work in a group. Look at the pictures. Read the idioms.
Guess the meanings.

Jack and Kate met in 1994. They both **had stars in their eyes**.

In 1996, Jack **popped the question**. Kate said yes.

Before they got married, Jack **got cold feet**. He was worried.

On June 15, Jack and Kate **tied the knot**. They were very happy.

One year later, their marriage was **on the rocks**. They had many problems.

Jack and Kate talked about their problems. It was **smooth sailing** after that.

Write a new sentence for each idiom. Read your sentences to the class.

3 Wrap up

Complete the **Self-assessment** on page 143.

Review

1 Listening

🔘 **Read** the questions. Then listen and circle the answers.

1. Where are Pablo and Marie?
   a. at a bus station
   (b.) at an airport

2. Why is Marie there?
   a. She just came back from Florida.
   b. She is meeting her parents.

3. How often does Marie visit her parents?
   a. every three months
   b. three times a year

4. Why is Pablo there?
   a. to meet Marie
   b. to meet his brother

5. How often does David visit?
   a. every weekend
   b. every vacation

6. How long does David usually stay?
   a. for three days
   b. for a week

Talk with a partner. Ask and answer the questions. Use complete sentences.

2 Grammar

A Write. Complete the story.

Christina's Last Vacation

Twice a year, Christina _____*takes*_____ a two-week vacation. Last
                              1. take

year, she ____*visited*____ her brother in Chicago. It ____*took*____
              2. visit   3. take

two days to get there by train. She and her brother ____*saw*____
                                                          4. see

a baseball game at Wrigley Field and ____*got*____ to a concert in
                                          5. go

Grant Park. It ____*been*____ a great vacation. Christina always
                    6. be

____*had*____ a good time with her brother.
    7. have

B Write. Look at the answers. Write the questions.

1. **A** How often *does Christina take a vacation* ?
   B Christina takes a vacation twice a year.

2. **A** When *did she visit her brother* ?
   B She visited her brother in Chicago last year.

3. **A** How long *did it take to get to Chicago*?
   B It took two days to get there.

4. **A** Where *did they see the baseball game*?
   B They saw a baseball game at Wrigley Field.

Talk with a partner. Ask and answer the questions.

3 Pronunciation: intonation in questions

A 💿 **Listen** to the intonation in these questions.

| Where is the train station? | Is the train station on Broadway or on Main Street? |

B 💿 **Listen and repeat.**

Wh- questions
A How often do you eat at a restaurant?
B Once a week.

Or questions
A Do you eat at a restaurant once a week or once a month?
B Once a week.

C **Talk** with a partner. Ask and answer the questions.

1. How often do you take a vacation? About a month.
2. Do you like to take a vacation in the summer or in the winter? in the summer.
3. When was your last vacation? October 10 2014.
4. Where did you go? South Carlinai
5. Did you go alone or with your family? whith my family.
6. What did you do there? took a trip

D **Write** five questions. Make at least two questions using *or.*

Do you take a bus or a train to school?

1. Did you go to the Fair or circus?
2. Did you like the dragon or the fireball?
3. Do you lik to ride the bus?
4. Is you favorite color pink?
5. Did you ride the train?

Talk with a partner. Ask and answer the questions.

| Do you take a bus or a train to school? | I take a bus. |

Shopping

1 Talk about the picture

A Look at the picture. What do you see?

B Point to: a customer • a piano • appliances • a sofa
furniture • a price tag • a salesperson • a stove

C Describe the furniture. How much do the items cost?

USED FURNITURE
BIGGEST SALE OF THE YEAR!

$105

$39

$705

$1,200

PIANOS

$99

$399

$215

$150

$25

$69

$199

$1,000

$22

Nick

SALE!
20% OFF

$400

WE HAVE THE
LOWEST PRICES

Denise

2 Listening

A **Listen.** What are Nick and Denise talking about? Write the letter of the conversation.

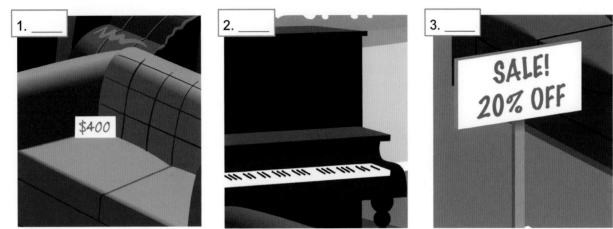

1. _____   2. _____   3. _____ $400   SALE! 20% OFF

B **Listen again.** Write *T* (true) or *F* (false).

Conversation A

1. Denise and Nick need furniture.   _T_

2. Denise and Nick bought a house two days ago.   _____

3. The furniture and appliances are 10 percent off.   _____

Conversation B

4. Denise likes the brown sofa.   _____

5. Nick wants a big sofa.   _____

6. The brown sofa is more expensive than the blue sofa.   _____

Conversation C

7. Denise and Nick need a piano.   _____

8. The upright piano is very old.   _____

9. The smaller piano is more expensive.   _____

Listen again. Check your answers.

C **Talk** with a partner. Ask and answer the questions.

1. What are some good ways to find furniture?
2. Did you ever buy furniture in this country?
3. What did you buy?

Culture note

Many stores in the U.S. sell furniture and appliances that are *not* new. The prices are cheaper. These stores are often called *used-furniture, thrift,* or *secondhand* stores.

Lesson B *The brown sofa is bigger.*

1 Grammar focus: comparatives

Statements

The brown sofa is	bigger.
	more expensive.

Comparatives

big → bigger
cheap → cheaper
heavy → heavier
small → smaller

comfortable → more comfortable
expensive → more expensive

good → better

For additional comparative adjectives, turn to page 151.

$1,000 $699

2 Practice

A Write. Complete the conversations. Use comparatives.

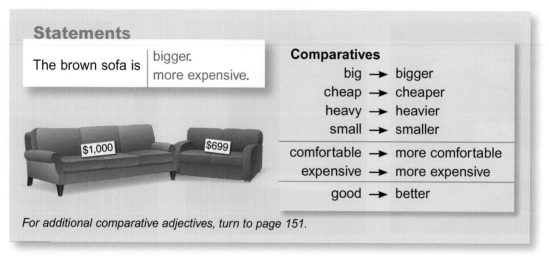

1. **A** Which sofa is more comfortable?

   B *The green striped sofa is more comfortable.*
   (green striped sofa / blue plaid sofa)

2. **A** Which chair is heavier?

   B The orange chair is heavier
   (orange chair / purple chair)

3. **A** Which refrigerator is more expensive?

   B The silver refrigerator is more expensive
   (white refrigerator / silver refrigerator)

4. **A** Which table is bigger?

   B The square table is bigger
   (square table / round table)

5. **A** Which stove is better?

   B The black stove is better
   (white stove / black stove)

Listen and repeat. Then practice with a partner.

$99 $399

B Talk with a partner. Change the **bold** words and make conversations.

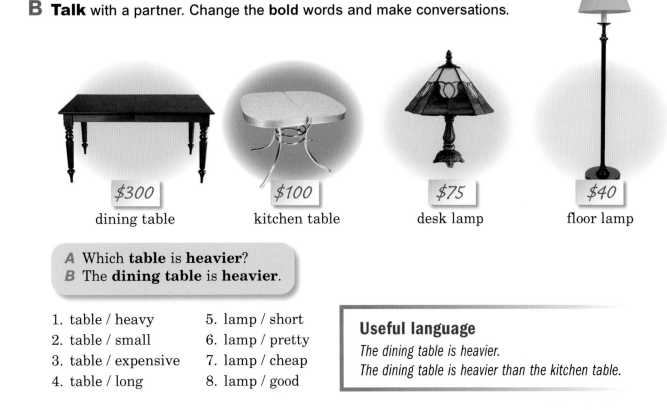

$300
dining table

$100
kitchen table

$75
desk lamp

$40
floor lamp

> *A* Which **table** is **heavier**?
> *B* The **dining table** is **heavier**.

1. table / heavy
2. table / small
3. table / expensive
4. table / long

5. lamp / short
6. lamp / pretty
7. lamp / cheap
8. lamp / good

Useful language

The dining table is heavier.
The dining table is heavier than the kitchen table.

3 Communicate

Talk with a partner. Compare the furniture in each store window.

Used Furniture

Perry's Thrift Shop

Secondhand Furniture

Greg's Used-Furniture Mart

> *A* I like the **lamp** at **Perry's Thrift Shop**.
> *B* Why?
> *A* It's **prettier**.

The yellow chair is the cheapest.

1 Grammar focus: superlatives

Statements

The blue chair is	cheap.
The red chair is	cheaper.
The yellow chair is	the cheapest.

Superlatives

big → the biggest
cheap → the cheapest
heavy → the heaviest
old → the oldest
small → the smallest

expensive → the most expensive

good → the best

For additional superlative adjectives, turn to page 151.

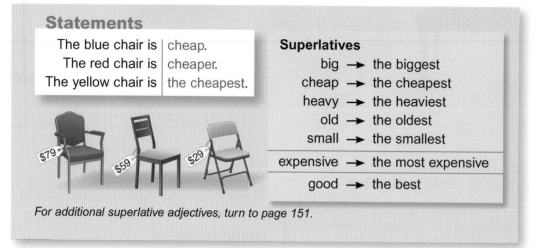

$79 $59 $29

2 Practice

A Write. Complete the conversations. Use superlatives.

$1,000 $75 $200

1. **A** Which TV is _____the cheapest_____ ?
   (cheap)
   B *The brown TV is the cheapest.*

2. **A** Which TV is __the heaviest__ ?
   tv is (heavy)
   B The brown, the heaviest

3. **A** Which TV is __more expensive__?
   (expensive)
   B The red tv is more expensive

4. **A** Which TV is __the oldest__ ?
   (old)
   B the brown tv is the oldest

5. **A** Which TV is __the_____ ?
   (small)
   B _____

6. **A** Which TV is _____ ?
   (big)
   B _____

Listen and repeat. Then practice with a partner.

B **Write.** Complete the conversation. Use superlatives.

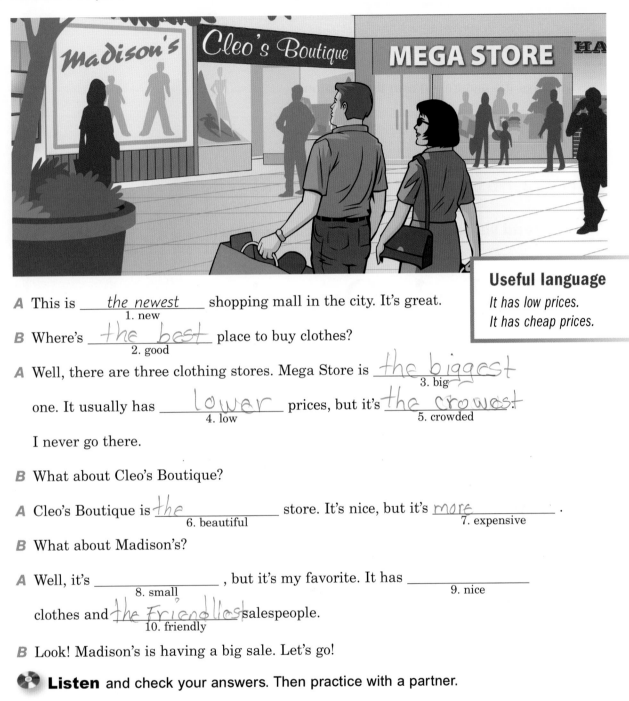

A This is ___the newest___ shopping mall in the city. It's great.
  1. new

B Where's ___the best___ place to buy clothes?
  2. good

Useful language
It has low prices.
It has cheap prices.

A Well, there are three clothing stores. Mega Store is ___the biggest___
  3. big

  one. It usually has ___lower___ prices, but it's ___the crowdest___.
  4. low   5. crowded

  I never go there.

B What about Cleo's Boutique?

A Cleo's Boutique is ___the___ store. It's nice, but it's ___more___ .
  6. beautiful   7. expensive

B What about Madison's?

A Well, it's _____ , but it's my favorite. It has _____
  8. small   9. nice

  clothes and ___the friendliest___ salespeople.
  10. friendly

B Look! Madison's is having a big sale. Let's go!

🔘 **Listen** and check your answers. Then practice with a partner.

3 Communicate

Talk in a group. Ask and answer the questions about places in your community.

1. Which clothing store is the biggest?
2. Which clothing store has the lowest prices?
3. Which supermarket is the cheapest?
4. Which restaurant is the best?

Reading

1 Before you read

Look at the picture. Answer the questions.

1. Who is the woman?
2. What did she buy?

2 Read

SELF-STUDY
AUDIO CD

Read the newspaper article. Listen and read again.

Today's Question
What's the best thing you ever bought?

The best thing I ever bought was an old piano. I bought it in a used-furniture store last month. It was the most beautiful piano in the store, but it wasn't very expensive. It has a beautiful sound. Now my two children are taking piano lessons. I love to hear music in the house.

Denise Robinson
Charleston, SC

I bought a used van five years ago. I used my van to help people move and to deliver stoves and refrigerators from a secondhand appliance store. I made a lot of money with that van. Now I have my own business. That van is the best thing I ever bought.

Sammy Chin
Myrtle Beach, SC

> Guess the meaning of new words from other words nearby.
> *appliances = stoves, refrigerators*

3 After you read

Write. Answer the questions about the article.

1. What did Denise buy? *She bought an old piano.*
2. What did Sammy buy? _____
3. Who is taking piano lessons? _____
4. Who has a business? _____
5. Which was probably more expensive – the piano or the van? _____

_____

4 Picture dictionary · Furniture

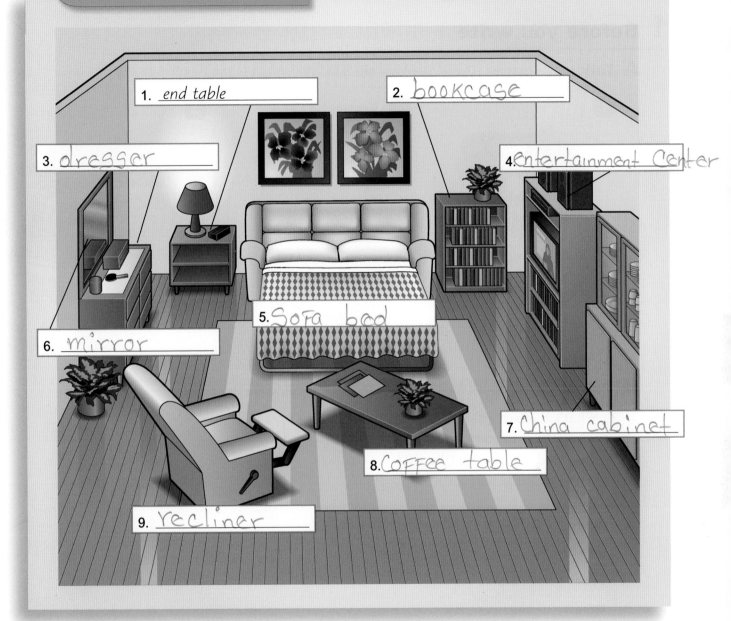

1. _end table_
2. _bookcase_
3. _dresser_
4. _entertainment center_
5. _sofa bed_
6. _mirror_
7. _china cabinet_
8. _coffee table_
9. _recliner_

SELF-STUDY
AUDIO CD

A **Write** the words in the picture dictionary. Then listen and repeat.

bookcase	dresser	mirror
china cabinet	end table	recliner
coffee table	entertainment center	sofa bed

B **Talk** with a partner. Change the **bold** words and make conversations.

> **A** Which is **bigger**, the **coffee table** or the **end table**?
> **B** The **coffee table** is **bigger**.

> **A** Do you like the **bookcase**?
> **B** **Yes**, I **do**. It's **nicer** than my **bookcase**.

1 Before you write

A **Talk** with a partner. These blankets are gifts. Which gift is the best? Tell why.

1 **2** **3**

B **Talk** with three classmates. Ask questions and complete the chart.

1. What's the best gift you ever received?
2. Who gave it to you?
3. When did you receive this gift?
4. Why was it the best gift?

Name	Paolo			
Best gift	a trip to Brazil			
From	his wife			
When	last summer			
Why	because he saw his parents again			

Talk. Share your information with the class.

> Paolo's best gift was a trip to Brazil last summer. His wife gave it to him. It was the best gift because he saw his parents again.

C **Read** the story. Complete the sentences.

ago	heart	necklace
birthday	mother	store

The Best Gift

The best gift I ever received was a _____necklace_____ . My
_____mother_____ bought it in a jewelry _____store_____ .
1   3
The necklace was in the shape of a _____heart_____ . She gave
              4
it to me for my _____birthday_____ a long time _____ago_____ .
      5   6
My mother said it was her heart. It was the best gift because it

was from her.

D **Write.** Answer the questions about yourself.

1. What is the best gift you ever received? _an expensive necklace_
2. Who gave it to you? _my daughter_
3. Why did you receive it? _It was my birthday_
4. Did the gift come from a store? _Yes, it did_
5. When did you receive this gift? _a year ago_
6. Why was it the best gift? _because my daughter gave it to me_

2 Write

Write a paragraph about the best gift you ever received.
Use Exercises 1C and 1D to help you.

> Use *because* to answer the question
> *Why* and to give a reason.
> *It was the best gift **because** it was beautiful.*

3 After you write

A **Read** your paragraph to a partner.

B **Check** your partner's paragraph.
- What was the gift? _a neckles_
- Why was it the best gift? _because my daughter gave it to me_
- Did your partner use *because* to say why?

Another view

1 Life-skills reading

Al's Discount Furniture
2100 Willow Boulevard
Charleston, SC 29401
(843) 555-0936

SALES RECEIPT

Sold to:
Nick Robinson
2718 Central Avenue
Charleston, SC 29412

Item #	Description	Price
1.	Blue sofa	$699.00
2.	Coffee table	$295.00
3.	Table lamp	$39.95
4.	Bookcase	$149.00
	Subtotal	$1,182.95
	Sales tax 7.5%	$88.72
	TOTAL	**$1,271.67**
	VISTA/MASTERCHARGE	$1,271.67

No refunds or exchanges after 30 days.

A Read the questions. Look at the sales receipt. Circle the answers.

1. Which is the cheapest item?
   a. the blue sofa
   b. the bookcase
   c. the coffee table
   d. the table lamp

2. Which is the most expensive item?
   a. the blue sofa
   b. the bookcase
   c. the coffee table
   d. the table lamp

3. When can a customer *not* exchange an item?
   a. after 7 days
   b. after 15 days
   c. before 30 days
   d. after 30 days

4. What is the total of the receipt?
   a. $88.72
   b. $699.00
   c. $1,182.95
   d. $1,271.67

B Talk with a partner. Ask and answer the questions.

1. What percent is the sales tax on the receipt for Al's Discount Furniture? 7.5%
2. What percent is the sales tax in your town or city?
3. Did you buy any furniture this year? What did you buy? a dresser

2 Fun with language

A Work in a group. Complete the chart with names of people in your group.

1. Who has the oldest child?	*Teresa*
2. Who has the shortest first name?	Edna/Elia
3. Who has the longest last name?	My last name
4. Who has the most brothers and sisters?	Elia
5. Who is the tallest?	Afifa
6. Who is the youngest?	Marta
7. Who has the longest hair?	Marta
8. Who has the smallest shoe size?	Elia
9. Who is wearing the biggest ring?	I don't know
10. Who has the oldest pet?	I don't know

Talk. Share your information with the class.

> Teresa has the oldest child. Her son is 24 years old.

B Write. Think of a piece of furniture in your home. Write it on the paper.

sofa   bookcase
mirror

Work with a partner. Ask and answer questions to guess the pieces of furniture. You can only answer *Yes* or *No*.

A Is it in your bedroom?
B No.
A Is it in your living room?
B Yes.
A Do you sit on it?
B Yes.
A Is it a sofa?
B Yes.

Is it in the living room?
No
Is it in your kitchen?
Yes
Do you sit on it?
No
Is it a table?
Yes.

3 Wrap up

Complete the **Self-assessment** on page 144.

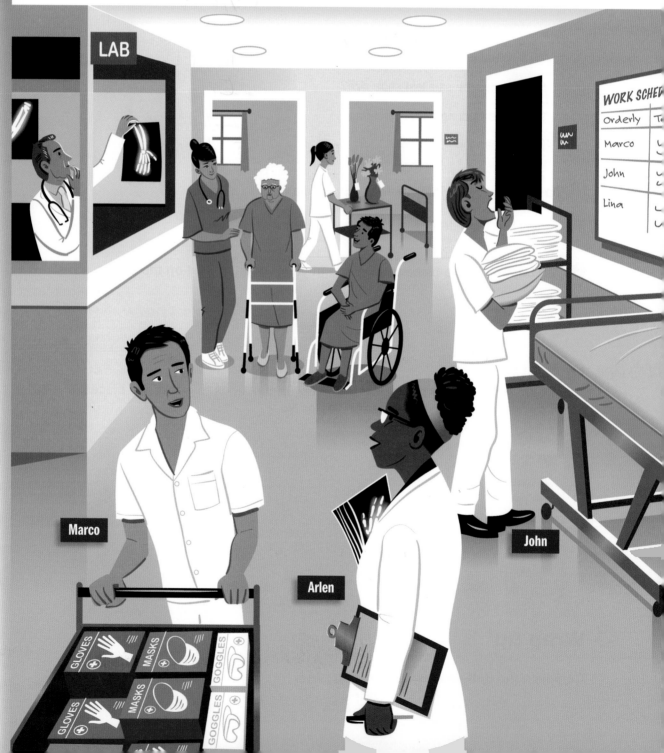

Lesson A *Get ready*

1 Talk about the picture

A Look at the picture. What do you see?

B Point to: a lab • linens • a patient • a walker

supplies • co-workers • an orderly • a wheelchair

C Look at these people. What are they doing?

LAB

WORK SCHE[W]

Orderly	T[o]
Marco	
John	
Lina	

Marco

Arlen

John

2 Listening

  A 🔊 **Listen.** What is Marco talking about? Write the letter of the conversation.

1. ____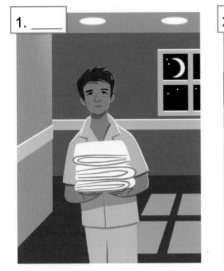

2. ____

Human Resources Office

3. ____

To do:

Deliver flowers ☑
Pick up X-rays ☑
Deliver linens ☑
Make beds ☑

B 🔊 **Listen again.** Write *T* (true) or *F* (false).

Conversation A

1. Marco picked up X-rays this morning. ___*T*___

2. Marco delivered linens to the third floor. ____

3. Marco needs to prepare rooms on the second floor. ____

Conversation B

4. John is tired. ____

5. Marco worked the night shift. ____

6. Marco wants to go back to school. ____

Conversation C

7. Suzanne works in Human Resources. ____

8. Marco wants to be a nurse. ____

9. Marco wants to work full-time. ____

Listen again. Check your answers.

> **Culture note**
> People who work at night work the *night shift*.

C **Talk** with a partner. Ask and answer the questions.

1. Do you have a job? What do you do?
2. Did you have a job before? What did you do?
3. What job do you want in the future?

Where did you go last night?

1 Grammar focus: *What* and *Where* questions and simple past

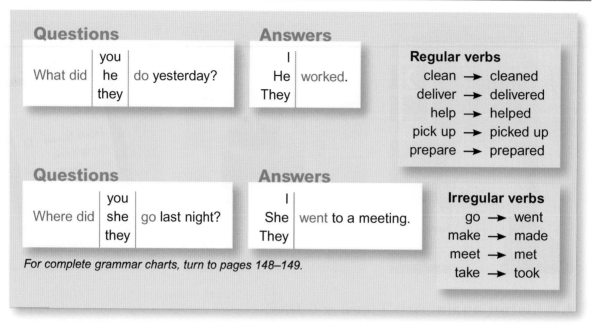

Questions

| What did | you
he
they | do yesterday? |

Answers

| I
He
They | worked. |

Regular verbs

clean → cleaned
deliver → delivered
help → helped
pick up → picked up
prepare → prepared

Questions

| Where did | you
she
they | go last night? |

Answers

| I
She
They | went to a meeting. |

Irregular verbs

go → went
make → made
meet → met
take → took

For complete grammar charts, turn to pages 148–149.

2 Practice

A Write. Complete the conversations. Use *What* or *Where* and the simple past.

1. **A** ___*What*___ did Linda do after breakfast?
   B She ____*made*____ the beds.
                (make)

2. **A** _____ did Brenda and Leo do this morning?
   B They _____ patients in the reception area.
                    (pick up)

3. **A** _____ did Trevor do this morning?
   B He _____ X-rays.
               (deliver)

4. **A** _____ did Jill and Brad take the linens?
   B They _____ the linens to the second floor.
                  (take)

5. **A** _____ did Felix do yesterday?
   B He _____ patients with their walkers
               (help)
   and wheelchairs.

6. **A** _____ did Juan and Ivana go after work?
   B They _____ to the coffee shop across the street.
                  (go)

Listen and repeat. Then practice with a partner.

B **Talk** with a partner. Change the **bold** words and make conversations.

> **A** Where did Rosa go at **8:00**?
> **B** She went to the **coffee shop**.
> **A** What did she do there?
> **B** She **ate breakfast**.

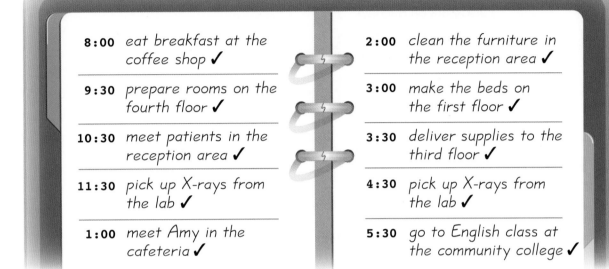

8:00 eat breakfast at the coffee shop ✓	**2:00** clean the furniture in the reception area ✓
9:30 prepare rooms on the fourth floor ✓	**3:00** make the beds on the first floor ✓
10:30 meet patients in the reception area ✓	**3:30** deliver supplies to the third floor ✓
11:30 pick up X-rays from the lab ✓	**4:30** pick up X-rays from the lab ✓
1:00 meet Amy in the cafeteria ✓	**5:30** go to English class at the community college ✓

3 Communicate

Talk with a partner. Ask questions. Write your partner's answers in the chart.

> **A** Rachel, where did you go last weekend?
> **B** I went to the mall.
> **A** What did you do?
> **B** I ate lunch and went shopping.
> **A** Did you have fun?
> **B** Yes, I did.

	Where?	**What?**
last weekend	the mall	ate lunch and went shopping
last Monday		
this morning		
last summer		
last night		

I work on Saturdays and Sundays.

1 Grammar focus: conjunctions *and, or, but*

Statements

I work on Saturdays. I also work on Sundays.	I work on Saturdays **and** Sundays.
Sometimes he works on Saturdays. Sometimes he works on Sundays.	He works on Saturdays **or** Sundays.
She works on Saturdays. She doesn't work on Sundays.	She works on Saturdays, **but** she doesn't work on Sundays.

2 Practice

A Write. Combine the sentences. Use *and, or,* or *but.*

1. Sometimes Irene eats Chinese food for lunch. Sometimes she eats Mexican food for lunch.

   Irene eats Chinese food or Mexican food for lunch.

2. Tito works the day shift. Tito also works the night shift.

   _____

3. Marco had an interview. He didn't get the job.

   _____

4. Brian likes his co-workers. He doesn't like his schedule.

   _____

5. Erica takes care of her children. She also takes care of her grandmother.

   _____

6. Carl cleaned the carpets. He didn't make the beds.

   _____

7. Sometimes Kate works in New York. Sometimes she works in San Diego.

   _____

8. Ilya speaks Russian at home. He also speaks Russian at work.

   _____

Listen and repeat. Check your answers.

B **Talk** with a partner. Change the **bold** words and make conversations.

Jill

go to work / feel well

go to a meeting / take notes

write a letter / finish it

> **A** What did Jill do yesterday?
> **B** She **went to work**, but she didn't **feel well**.

Al

write reports / check e-mail

make copies / deliver mail

answer calls / take messages

> **A** What did Al do this morning?
> **B** He **wrote reports** and **checked e-mail**.

You

in a restaurant / at my desk

in the cafeteria / outside

at home / in my car

> **A** Where do you eat lunch?
> **B** I eat lunch **in a restaurant** or **at my desk**.

3 Communicate

Talk with a partner. Make statements with *and*, *or*, or *but*.

> Last night, I watched TV and did my homework. What about you?

> I did my homework, but I didn't watch TV.

Reading

1 Before you read

Look at the picture. Answer the questions.

1. Who are these people?
2. What are they doing?

2 Read

SELF-STUDY
AUDIO CD **Read** the letter of recommendation. Listen and read again.

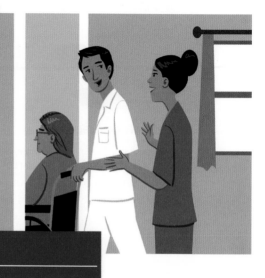

Valley ✚ Hospital

Dear Mr. O'Hara:

    I am happy to write this letter of recommendation for Marco Alba. Marco started working at Valley Hospital as an orderly in 2003. He takes patients from their rooms to the lab, delivers X-rays, and takes flowers and mail to patients. He also delivers linens and supplies. He is an excellent worker, and his co-workers like him very much.

    We are sorry to lose Marco. He wants to go to school and needs to work part-time, but we don't have a part-time job for him right now. I recommend Marco very highly. Please contact me for more information.

Sincerely,

Suzanne Briggs

Suzanne Briggs
Human Resources Assistant

> Look through the text quickly for specific information, like names and dates.
> *Marco Alba   2003*

> **Culture note**
> Teachers and employers often write letters of recommendation to help you get a job or get into a school.

3 After you read

Write. Answer the questions about Marco.

1. When did Marco start his job at Valley Hospital? *He started his job in 2003.*
2. What does he do there? _____
3. Why is Marco leaving? _____
4. Who wrote the letter? _____

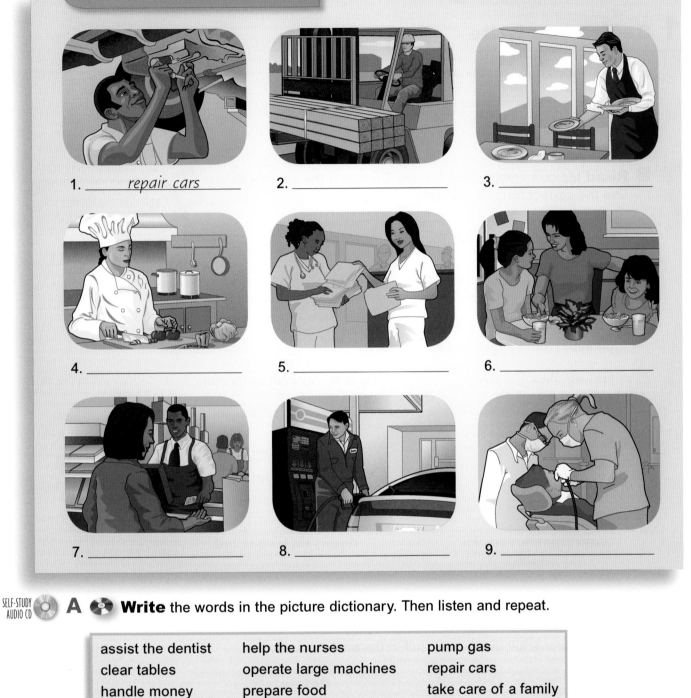

1. _repair cars_
2. _____
3. _____
4. _____
5. _____
6. _____
7. _____
8. _____
9. _____

A **Write** the words in the picture dictionary. Then listen and repeat.

assist the dentist	help the nurses	pump gas
clear tables	operate large machines	repair cars
handle money	prepare food	take care of a family

B **Talk** with a partner. Match the pictures with the jobs.

an auto mechanic	a construction worker	a gas station attendant
a busboy	a cook	a housewife
a cashier	a dental assistant	an orderly

He repairs cars.   He's an auto mechanic.

Lesson E *Writing*

1 Before you write

A Talk with a partner. Ask and answer the questions.

1. What are some of your duties at home?
2. What are some of your duties at your job?
3. What were some of your duties at your last job?

B Read Marco's employment history. Complete the sentences. Use the correct form of the verb.

> Capitalize the names of businesses.
> *Valley Hospital*

☤ Employment History: Marco Alba

Marco Alba is an orderly. He ___*works*___ at Valley Hospital. He
                               1. work

started in 2003. He _____ many duties. He _____
               2. have   3. take

patients from their rooms to the lab. He _____ X-rays, linens,
                                          4. deliver

and supplies. He also _____ flowers and mail to patients.
                            5. take

From 2001 to 2003, Marco _____ at Sam's Soup and
                             6. work

Sandwich Shop. He _____ a busboy. He _____ the
                    7. be   8. clean

floor and _____ dirty dishes. From 2000 to 2001, he
         9. pick up

_____ at Fratelli's Construction Company. He _____ a
10. work   11. be

construction worker. He _____ repairs on houses and
                       12. make

_____ large machines.
13. operate

C Write Marco's job duties now and in the past.

Now	Before
1. He takes patients from their rooms to the lab.	1.
2.	2.
3.	3.
	4.

D Write. Answer the questions about yourself.

Do you have a job? Yes?
Answer these questions.

1. What is your job?

_____

_____

2. Where do you work?

_____

_____

3. What are your duties?

_____

_____

4. Did you have a job before?
   What jobs did you have?

_____

_____

5. Where did you work?

_____

_____

6. What were your duties?

_____

_____

Do you have a job? No?
Answer these questions.

1. Where do you study?

_____

_____

2. What do you study at school?

_____

_____

3. Did you have a job before?
   What jobs did you have?

_____

_____

4. Where did you work?

_____

_____

5. What were your duties?

_____

_____

2 Write

Write your employment history. Use Exercises 1B, 1C, and 1D to help you.

3 After you write

A Read your employment history to a partner.

B Check your partner's employment history.

- What are the jobs?
- What are the duties?
- Do the names of businesses start with capital letters?

Another view

1 Life-skills reading

LARRY'S DISCOUNT STORE – WEEKLY TIME SHEET

Employee: *Iara da Silva*   Social Security Number: *000-99-0531*
Rate: *$9.00/hour*

DAY	DATE	TIME IN	TIME OUT	TIME IN	TIME OUT	HOURS
MONDAY	8/7	9:00 A.M.	12:00 NOON	1:00 P.M.	4:00 P.M.	6
TUESDAY	8/8	8:30 A.M.	12:30 P.M.	1:30 P.M.	5:30 P.M.	8
WEDNESDAY	8/9	9:00 A.M.	2:00 P.M.	3:00 P.M.	7:00 P.M.	9
THURSDAY	8/10	7:30 A.M.	12:30 P.M.	1:30 P.M.	3:30 P.M.	7
FRIDAY	8/11	9:00 A.M.	12:00 NOON	1:00 P.M.	5:00 P.M.	7
TOTAL HOURS						37

I have worked these hours. I understand that false information will result in my termination with the company.

Employee's signature *Iara da Silva*   Date: *8/25*

Supervisor's signature *Helen Wilson*   Date: *8/25*

A **Read** the questions. Look at the time sheet. Circle the answers.

1. What is Iara's hourly rate?
   a. 9:00–5:00
   b. 8 hours
   c. $9
   d. $37

2. When did Iara start work on Tuesday?
   a. 7:30 a.m.
   b. 8:30 a.m.
   c. 9:00 a.m.
   d. 9:30 a.m.

3. When did Iara leave work on Friday?
   a. 3:30 p.m.
   b. 4:30 p.m.
   c. 5:00 p.m.
   d. 5:30 p.m.

4. What day did Iara start work at 7:30?
   a. Monday
   b. Tuesday
   c. Wednesday
   d. Thursday

B **Talk** with a partner. Ask and answer the questions.

1. When do you start school or work?
2. What days do you study or work?
3. How many hours do you study or work each day?
4. Do you like your schedule? Why or why not?

2 Fun with language

A Work with a partner. Complete the sentences. Share them with the class.

Use *and*:

1. I want to buy some new shoes and _____ .

2. I need to clean my house and _____ .

3. I can speak English and _____ .

Use *or*:

4. I want to work in an office or _____ .

5. I need to save money for a car or _____ .

6. I can work on Saturday or _____ .

Use *but*:

7. I want to work on the weekends, but _____ .

8. I want to buy a new car, but _____ .

9. I can speak English, but _____ .

B Work in a group. Look at these expressions. What do they mean?
Talk about them in your group.

1 I can't **make up my mind**.

2 Can you **give me a hand**?

3 There's a lot of **junk mail**.

4 That test was a **piece of cake**.

3 Wrap up

Complete the **Self-assessment** on page 144.

Review

1 Listening

🔘 **Read** the questions. Then listen and circle the answers.

1. What does Yuri do?
   - (a.) He's a salesperson.
   - b. He's a manager.

2. Why did the Chans want a new sofa?
   - a. Their sofa wasn't clean.
   - b. Their sofa wasn't comfortable.

3. Which sofa was cheaper?
   - a. the first sofa
   - b. the second sofa

4. Why did they like the second sofa?
   - a. It was bigger and more comfortable.
   - b. It was nicer and more expensive.

5. What did Mr. and Mrs. Chan buy?
   - a. a sofa and two lamps
   - b. a sofa and an entertainment center

6. Where did Yuri go after work?
   - a. to a supermarket
   - b. to a restaurant

Talk with a partner. Ask and answer the questions. Use complete sentences.

2 Grammar

A Write. Complete the story.

Vanessa's Last Job

Last year, Vanessa _____worked_____ the day shift at the Hometown
                         1. work

Hotel. First, she _____ to the supply room at 8:00 a.m. Next,
                       2. go

she _____ her cart to the third floor. Then, she _____
         3. take   4. make

the beds. After that, she _____ the rooms and _____
                               5. clean   6. pick up

dirty linens. Vanessa's job _____ easy, but she liked it because
                                  7. not / be

she _____ a lot of nice people.
        8. meet

B Write. Look at the answers. Write the questions.

1. **A** Where _did Vanessa work last year_ ?
   B Vanessa worked at the Hometown Hotel last year.

2. **A** What shift _____ ?
   B She worked the day shift.

3. **A** When _____ ?
   B She went to the supply room at 8:00 a.m.

4. **A** Where _____ ?
   B She took her cart to the third floor.

Talk with a partner. Ask and answer the questions.

3 Pronunciation: the -s ending in the simple present

A **Listen** to the -s ending in these simple present verbs.

/s/	/z/	/ɪz/
talks	is	watches
makes	has	fixes

B **Listen and repeat.**

/s/	/z/	/ɪz/
looks	buys	relaxes
shops	delivers	teaches
speaks	plays	fixes

C **Listen** and check (✓) the correct column.

	/s/	/z/	/ɪz/		/s/	/z/	/ɪz/
1. drives	☐	☐	☐	5. takes	☐	☐	☐
2. gets	☐	☐	☐	6. pushes	☐	☐	☐
3. goes	☐	☐	☐	7. sleeps	☐	☐	☐
4. uses	☐	☐	☐	8. needs	☐	☐	☐

D **Write** six verbs from Units 7 and 8 in the present tense. Check (✓) the correct column for the -s ending.

	/s/	/z/	/ɪz/		/s/	/z/	/ɪz/
1.	☐	☐	☐	4.	☐	☐	☐
2.	☐	☐	☐	5.	☐	☐	☐
3.	☐	☐	☐	6.	☐	☐	☐

Talk with a partner. Read the words.

Lesson A Get ready

1 Talk about the picture

A Look at the picture. What do you see?

B Point to: a dishwasher • a leak • a lightbulb • a lock
a dryer • garbage • a sink • a washing machine

C Look at the woman. What's she doing?

Stella

2 Listening

SELF-STUDY
AUDIO CD

A **Listen.** Who is Stella talking to? Write the letter of the conversation.

1. ____

2. ____

3. ____

SELF-STUDY
AUDIO CD

B **Listen again.** Write *T* (true) or *F* (false).

Conversation A

1. Stella lives in Apartment 4B.   *T*

2. Stella is talking to a plumber.   ____

3. Don Brown is a neighbor.   ____

Conversation B

4. Stella wants to speak to her husband.   ____

5. Don Brown will come in one hour.   ____

6. Stella will unlock the door for the plumber.   ____

Conversation C

7. Russell wants Stella to call a neighbor.   ____

8. Stella already called the plumber.   ____

9. Stella is going to school.   ____

Listen again. Check your answers.

C **Talk** with a partner. Ask and answer the questions.

1. Who fixes things in your home?
2. Did you ever need to call a plumber or other repair person?
3. Who did you call?
4. What happened?

Lesson B *Which one do you recommend?*

1 Grammar focus: *Which* questions and simple present

	Questions				
Which	plumber	do	you	recommend?	
	electrician	does	he		
	one	do	they		

	Answers		
I	recommend	Home Repair.
He	recommends	
They	recommend	

For a complete grammar chart, turn to page 147.

2 Practice

A Write. Complete the conversations. Use *Which* and the simple present.

HARRISON'S PLUMBING SERVICE
FAST AND PROFESSIONAL
- $100 AN HOUR
- OPEN 24 HOURS A DAY / 7 DAYS A WEEK
- CLEAN
- 30 YEARS OF EXPERIENCE

555-7407

BROWN'S PLUMBING SERVICE   555-4564
Complete plumbing service
- $50 an hour
- Licensed
- 15 years of experience
- Insured

1. **A** *Which plumber do you recommend* ?
   B I recommend Brown's Plumbing Service. It's cheaper.
2. **A** _____ ?
   B He recommends Harrison's Plumbing Service. It's clean.
3. **A** _____ ?
   B They recommend Brown's Plumbing Service. It's licensed.
4. **A** _____ ?
   B She recommends Brown's Plumbing Service. It's insured.
5. **A** _____ ?
   B They recommend Harrison's Plumbing Service. It's more experienced.
6. **A** _____ ?
   B He recommends Harrison's Plumbing Service. It's open 24 hours a day.

> **Culture note**
> Plumbers and electricians are usually licensed. You can ask to see their license.

🔘 **Listen and repeat.** Then practice with a partner.

B **Talk** with a partner. Change the **bold** words and make conversations.

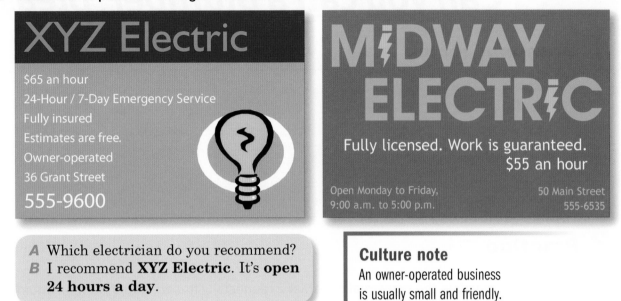

A Which electrician do you recommend?
B I recommend **XYZ Electric**. It's **open 24 hours a day**.

Culture note
An owner-operated business
is usually small and friendly.

1. open 24 hours a day
2. fully licensed
3. owner-operated
4. on Main Street
5. fully insured
6. cheaper

3 Communicate

Write. Answer the questions about your community.

1. Which supermarket do you like? _____

2. Which restaurant do you recommend? _____

3. Which drugstore do you recommend? _____

4. Which gas station do you suggest? _____

5. Which bank do you like? _____

6. Which department store do you suggest? _____

7. Which dentist do you like? _____

8. Which hospital do you recommend? _____

Talk with your classmates. Ask and answer questions about your community.

Which supermarket do you like?

I like SaveMore Supermarket on Broadway. It's clean.

I like Acme Supermarket. It's cheap.

Useful language
I recommend . . .
I suggest . . .
I like . . .

Lesson C *Can you call a plumber, please?*

1 Grammar focus: requests with *Can, Could, Will, Would*

Questions

Can Could Will Would	you	call a plumber, please?

2 Practice

A Write. Complete the conversations. Make requests with *can*, *could*, *will*, or *would*.

1.   2.   3.

fix the dryer   unclog the sink   clean the bathroom

4.   5.   6.

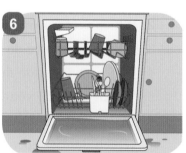

fix the lock   change the lightbulb   repair the dishwasher

1. **A** Could _you fix the dryer, please_ ?
   B Yes, of course.
2. **A** Can _____ ?
   B No, not now. Maybe later.
3. **A** Would _____ ?
   B Sorry, I can't right now.
4. **A** Will _____ ?
   B Sure. I'd be happy to.
5. **A** Could _____ ?
   B Yes, of course.
6. **A** Would _____ ?
   B Sure. I'd be happy to.

🔘 **Listen and repeat.** Then practice with a partner.

B Talk with a partner. Change the **bold** words and make conversations.

A Can you **fix the window**, please?
B Yes, of course.

1. fix the window
2. repair the refrigerator
3. unclog the sink
4. fix the toilet

A Would you **fix the stove**, please?
B Sorry, I can't right now.

5. fix the stove
6. fix the light
7. call an electrician
8. repair the lock

3 Communicate

Write. What are some problems in your home or in a friend's home? Make a list of requests for the landlord.

> Requests for the landlord
>
> 1. fix the window

Culture note
A tenant rents an apartment or house from the landlord. The landlord is the owner.

Talk. Role-play with a partner. One person is the tenant. The other is the landlord.

Tenant Could you fix the window, please?
Landlord Yes, of course. I'll be there tomorrow.

Useful language
Yes, of course.
Sure. I'd be happy to.
No, not now. Maybe later.
Sorry, I can't right now.

1 Before you read

Look at the picture. Answer the questions.

1. Who is the woman?
2. What's the problem?

2 Read

SELF-STUDY
AUDIO CD

Read Stella's notice. Listen and read again.

Attention, tenants:

Do you have problems in your apartment?
Is anyone fixing them?

- Many tenants have broken windows.
- Tenants on the third floor have no lights in the hall.
- A tenant on the second floor has a leaking ceiling.
- Tenants on the first floor smell garbage every day.

I'm really upset! We need to get together and write a letter of complaint to the manager of the building.

Come to a meeting Friday night at 7:00 p.m. in Apartment 4B.

Stella Taylor, Tenant 4B

> Sometimes it is not necessary to know the exact meaning of a word. It is enough to know if the meaning is positive (good) or negative (not good).
>
> *upset, complaint* = negative

3 After you read

Write. Answer the questions about Stella's notice.

1. Which tenant has a leaking ceiling? <u>*A tenant on the second floor.*</u>
2. Which tenants have no lights in the hall? _____
3. Which tenants smell garbage? _____
4. What does Stella want to write? _____
5. Where is the meeting? _____

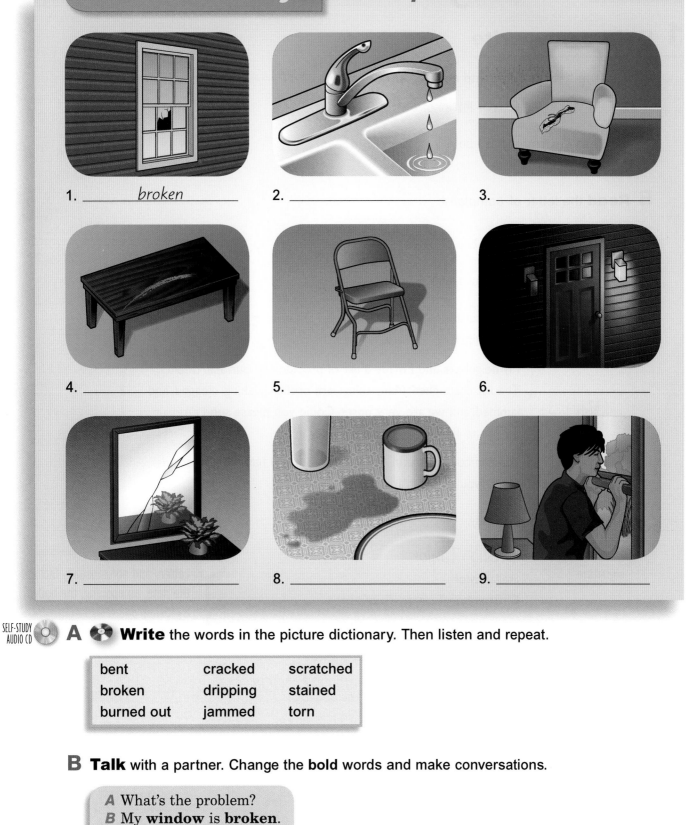

1. _____broken_____
2. _____
3. _____

4. _____
5. _____
6. _____

7. _____
8. _____
9. _____

SELF-STUDY AUDIO CD

A **Write** the words in the picture dictionary. Then listen and repeat.

bent	cracked	scratched
broken	dripping	stained
burned out	jammed	torn

B **Talk** with a partner. Change the **bold** words and make conversations.

A What's the problem?
B My **window** is **broken**.
Could you fix it, please?
A Sure. I'll try.

1 Before you write

A Talk in a group. Ask and answer the questions.

1. Did you ever write a letter of complaint?
2. Who did you write to?
3. What did you write about?
4. What happened?

B Read the letter of complaint.

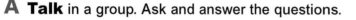

date — September 27, 2008

opening — Dear Building Manager:

body —

I am a tenant at 3914 Fifth Street. I am writing to you about many problems in the apartment building.

My neighbors and I made a list of problems in our apartments. The list is attached. Many things are broken, leaking, clogged, and jammed, and we are very upset. Could you please send a repair person to fix these things right away?

You can contact me in Apartment 4B if you have any questions. Thank you for your attention.

closing — Sincerely,

signature —

Stella Taylor
Stella Taylor
Chairperson, Tenants' Committee

> Letters and notes usually include the date, an opening, the body, a closing, and a signature.

C Write. Answer the questions about Stella's letter.

1. What is the date of this letter? *September 27, 2008.*
2. Who is the letter to? _____
3. Who is the letter from? _____
4. How many paragraphs are in the body of the letter? _____
5. What is the closing? _____

D **Write.** Read the list of problems. Complete the sentences.

broken	clogged	cracked	jammed	leaking	stained

Problems at 3914 Fifth Street

Apartment 1F
The carpet is _____ .
₁

Apartment 2C
The front door lock is _____ .
₂

Apartment 3A
The bedroom walls are _____ .
₃

Apartment 4B
The living room window is _____ .
₄

Apartment 5B
The refrigerator is _____ .
₅

Apartment 6D
The kitchen sink is _____ .
₆

E **Write** three sentences about problems in your apartment or house.

2 Write

Write a letter of complaint to your building manager or landlord.
Use Exercises 1B, 1D, and 1E to help you.

3 After you write

A **Read** your letter to a partner.

B **Check** your partner's letter.
- What are the problems?
- Who is the letter to?
- Does the letter have an opening and a closing?

Another view

1 Life-skills reading

A+ PLUMBING REPAIRS
Montague, New Jersey 07827

Free Estimates
We charge less and don't leave a mess!
(973) 555-2399   30-day guarantee on all repairs

CUSTOMER INVOICE 102051

CUSTOMER NAME *Victor Waters*

CUSTOMER ADDRESS *1872 Valley Street*
Newton, New Jersey 07860

SERVICE TECHNICIAN *Russ*

DESCRIPTION OF PROBLEM		ACTUAL COST
SINK CLOGGED		$30.00
BATHROOM SHOWER LEAKING		$35.00
DISHWASHER OVERFLOWED		$40.00
	TOTAL	$105.00

A Read the questions. Look at the invoice. Circle the answers.

1. How much is the total?
   a. $20.00
   b. $35.00
   c. $50.00
   d. $105.00

2. How much did it cost to fix the dishwasher?
   a. $30.00
   b. $35.00
   c. $40.00
   d. $105.00

3. What was leaking?
   a. the bathroom shower
   b. the dishwasher
   c. the sink
   d. the washing machine

4. Which repair was the most expensive?
   a. the bathroom shower
   b. the dishwasher
   c. the dryer
   d. the sink

B Talk with a partner. Ask and answer the questions.

1. What repair problems do you sometimes have?
2. Can you repair things in your home?
3. Do you have a friend or family member who can repair things?
4. What does that person help you with?

2 Fun with language

A Work with a partner. Match the home problems with the correct repair person.

1. a broken key _____
2. a burned-out light _____
3. a jammed window _____
4. an overflowing toilet _____
5. a stained wall _____

a. a carpenter
b. an electrician
c. a locksmith
d. a painter
e. a plumber

B Work in a group. Make a list. How many questions can you think of? Use *Can*, *Could*, *Will*, or *Would*.

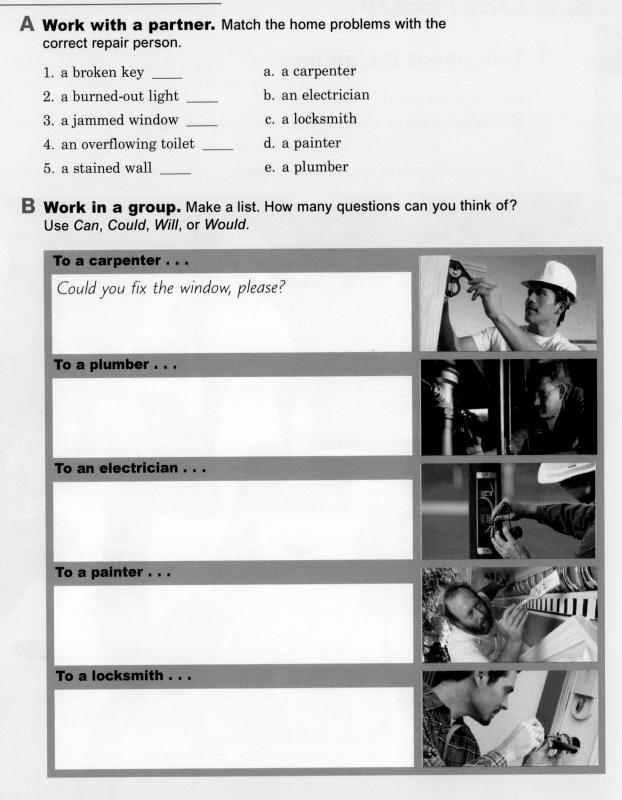

To a carpenter . . .

Could you fix the window, please?

To a plumber . . .

To an electrician . . .

To a painter . . .

To a locksmith . . .

3 Wrap up

Complete the **Self-assessment** on page 145.

Lesson **A** *Get ready*

1 Talk about the picture

A Look at the picture. What do you see?

B Point to: a card • a graduation cake • flowers • a guest
perfume • a piece of cake • balloons • a present

C Look at the people. What are they doing?

Celia

2 Listening

A **Listen.** Which gift is Celia talking about? Write the letter of the conversation.

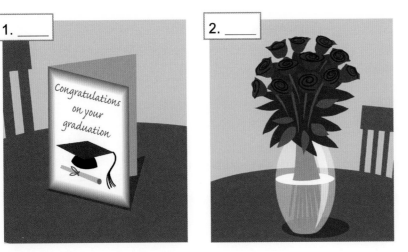

1. _____
2. _____

3. _____

B **Listen again.** Write *T* (true) or *F* (false).

Conversation A

1. Celia is having a birthday party.   *F*

2. Celia's mother made a cake.   _____

3. Ana gave Celia some flowers.   _____

Conversation B

4. Mrs. Campbell is a student.   _____

5. Celia started English class three years ago.   _____

6. Mrs. Campbell brought Celia a card.   _____

Conversation C

7. Sue brought her children to the party.   _____

8. Sue would like some water.   _____

9. Sue gave Celia some balloons.   _____

Listen again. Check your answers.

C **Talk** with a partner. Ask and answer the questions.

1. Does your family celebrate graduations?
2. How does your family celebrate?
3. What other special days does your family celebrate?

> **Culture note**
> People often celebrate someone's graduation with a party for family and friends.

Would you like some cake?

1 Grammar focus: *Would you like . . . ?*

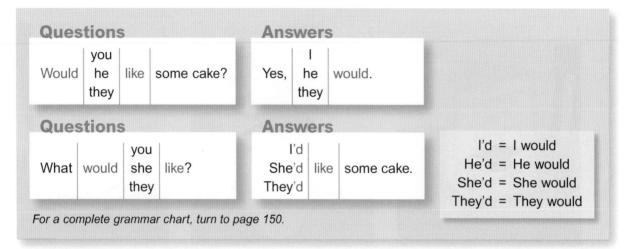

Questions

Would	you he they	like	some cake?

Answers

Yes,	I he they	would.

Questions

What	would	you she they	like?

Answers

I'd She'd They'd	like	some cake.

I'd = I would
He'd = He would
She'd = She would
They'd = They would

For a complete grammar chart, turn to page 150.

2 Practice

A Write. Complete the conversations.

1. **A** _____Would you like_____ a cup of coffee?
         (you)
   B Yes, __I would__ .

2. **A** _____ a balloon?
            (he)
   B Yes, _____ .

3. **A** _____ some ice cream?
            (she)
   B Yes, _____ .

4. **A** _____ a sandwich?
            (you)
   B Yes, _____ .

5. **A** _____ some salad?
            (they)
   B Yes, _____ .

6. **A** _____ a hot dog?
            (you)
   B Yes, _____ .

Listen and repeat. Then practice with a partner.

B **Talk** with a partner. Change the **bold** words and make conversations.

> *A* What would you like?
> *B* I'd like **some cake**, please.

1 some cake	**2** some fruit	**3** a piece of pie
4 some cheese	**5** a bottle of water	**6** some cookies
7 some soda	**8** some dessert	**9** a cup of tea

3 Communicate

Talk with a partner. Make conversations.

> *A* Would you like something to drink?
> *B* Yes, please.
> *A* What would you like?
> *B* I'd like some soda, please.
> *A* Would you like something to eat?
> *B* No, thank you. I'm full.

Useful language

Would you like something to drink?
Would you like something to eat?

Yes, please. / No, thank you. I'm full.

Tim gave Mary a present.

1 Grammar focus: direct and indirect objects

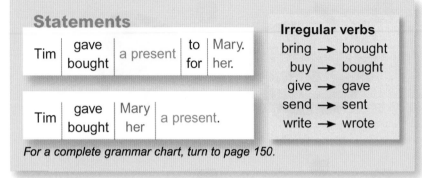

Statements

| Tim | gave / bought | a present | to / for | Mary. / her. |

| Tim | gave / bought | Mary / her | a present. |

Irregular verbs

bring → brought
buy → bought
give → gave
send → sent
write → wrote

For a complete grammar chart, turn to page 150.

2 Practice

A Write. Look at Joe's "to do" list. What did he do yesterday? Write sentences.

To do

✓ bring flowers to Sylvia
✓ buy a card for Nick
✓ write a letter to Pam
✓ buy a cake for Mary and Judy
✓ give roses to Eva
✓ send an invitation to Paul

1. *Joe brought flowers to Sylvia.*
2. _____
3. _____
4. _____
5. _____
6. _____

Write. Complete the conversations.

1. **A** What did Joe bring Sylvia?
   B *Joe brought Sylvia flowers.*

2. **A** What did Joe buy Nick?
   B _____

3. **A** What did Joe write Pam?
   B _____

4. **A** What did Joe buy Mary and Judy?
   B _____

5. **A** What did Joe give Eva?
   B _____

6. **A** What did Joe send Paul?
   B _____

Listen and repeat. Then practice with a partner.

B **Talk** with a partner. Change the **bold** words and make conversations.

some balloons

a card

some flowers

some cookies

some perfume

some books

A What did you give **Daniel**?
B I gave **him some balloons**.
A That's nice.

Useful language

he → him
she → her
they → them

3 Communicate

Write. Choose three classmates. Choose three items from your desk.
Give one thing to each classmate. Then complete the chart.

Classmates	Items
Anika	my _Ventures_ book
1.	
2.	
3.	

Talk with a partner. Share your information.

I gave Anika my _Ventures_ book.

I gave Rudy my pen.

Ask for your things back.

Anika, please give me my _Ventures_ book.

Rudy, please give me my pen.

Lesson D Reading

1 Before you read

Look at the picture. Answer the questions.

1. Who is the woman?
2. What is she doing?

2 Read

SELF-STUDY
AUDIO CD

Read the paragraph. Listen and read again.

> Look for examples of the main idea when you read. This paragraph is about gifts. Look for examples of all the gifts.

Thank you

Celia had a graduation party last Friday. Her husband sent invitations to Celia's teacher and to their relatives and friends. They all came to the party! Some guests brought gifts for Celia. Her teacher Mrs. Campbell gave her a card. Her Aunt Ana brought her flowers. Her friend Sue gave her some perfume. Her classmate Ruth brought her some cookies. After the party, Celia wrote them thank-you notes. Tomorrow, she is going to mail the thank-you notes at the post office.

Culture note
People often write thank-you notes. It is polite to thank someone for a gift.

3 After you read

Write. Answer the questions about Celia's graduation party.

1. When was Celia's graduation party? _Last Friday._ _____
2. Who came to the party? _____
3. What did Mrs. Campbell give Celia? _____
4. What did Sue give Celia? _____
5. What did Ruth bring Celia? _____
6. What is Celia going to do tomorrow? _____

1. _Thanksgiving_   2. _____   3. _____

4. _____   5. _____   6. _____

7. _____   8. _____   9. _____

SELF-STUDY
AUDIO CD   **A** **Write** the words in the picture dictionary. Then listen and repeat.

a baby shower	Independence Day	Thanksgiving
Halloween	Mother's Day	Valentine's Day
a housewarming	New Year's Eve	a wedding

B **Talk** with a partner. What special days do you celebrate?
How do you celebrate them?

Do you celebrate Thanksgiving?

Yes, we do. We always go to my mother-in-law's house for a big turkey dinner.

Writing

1 Before you write

A Talk with a partner. Ask and answer the questions.

1. Did you ever receive a thank-you note?
2. Did you ever send someone a thank-you note?
3. In other countries, when do people write thank-you notes?

B Read the thank-you note.

> Indent the paragraphs in an informal note.
> Don't indent the date or *Dear* _____ .

June 30, 2008

Dear Aunt Ana,

    Thank you for the lovely flowers you gave me for my graduation. They are beautiful! I really like the color of the roses. Red is my favorite color!

    Thank you so much for coming to my graduation party. I hope you had a good time.

                Love,
                Celia

Culture note
Use *Love* or *Best wishes* in a personal note.
Use *Sincerely* in a formal letter.

C Write. Answer the questions about Celia's note. Write complete sentences.

1. When did Celia write the note?
   Celia wrote the note on June 30, 2008.

2. Who did Celia write the note to?
   _____

3. What did Aunt Ana give Celia?
   _____

4. Why did Celia like the gift?
   _____

D Write. Complete the thank-you note.

Best wishes	birthday	color	Dear	fun	party	shirt	size

_____ ,
(today's date)

_____ John,
      1

    Thank you for the beautiful _____ you gave me for
                                   2

my _____ . It is just the right _____ .
      3   4

I also really like the _____ .
                       5

    Thank you so much for coming to my _____ . I hope
                                    6

you had _____ .
       7

_____ ,
      8
      Paula

E Write. Answer the questions.

1. When did a friend give you a present? _____

2. What is your friend's name? _____

3. What was the present? _____

4. Why did you like the present? _____

5. What was the celebration? _____

2 Write

Write a thank-you note to a friend for a gift. Use Exercises 1B, 1D, and 1E to help you.

3 After you write

A Read your note to a partner.

B Check your partner's note.
- What was the present?
- What was the celebration?
- Did your partner indent each paragraph?

Another view

1 Life-skills reading

**It's a party!
Please join us!**

Dear Will and Katya,

For: A New Year's Eve Party

Date: Wednesday, December 31

Time: 8:00 p.m. until 1:00 a.m.

Place: Tom and Luisa's

76 North Street, Apt. 6A

RSVP: (813) 555-1234 by December 15

Please bring something to drink.
No children, please!
Hope you can come!

A Read the questions. Look at the invitation. Circle the answers.

1. Who is giving the party?
   a. Luisa
   b. Tom and Luisa
   c. Will and Katya
   d. Will and Luisa

2. When do people need to say *yes* or *no* to the invitation?
   a. before December 15
   b. after December 15
   c. on December 31
   d. after December 31

3. What time will the party begin?
   a. 8:00 a.m.
   b. 1:00 p.m.
   c. 8:00 p.m.
   d. 1:00 a.m.

4. What should people bring to the party?
   a. something to drink
   b. something to eat
   c. their children
   d. nothing

B Talk in a group. Ask and answer the questions.

1. Do you like to go to parties? Do you like to give parties?
2. Do you usually bring something to a party? What?
3. Tell about the last party you went to.

2 Fun with language

A Work with a partner. Read the clues. Fill in the blanks.

baby shower	Halloween	New Year's Eve
birthday	housewarming	Valentine's Day
graduation party	Independence Day	wedding

1. July 4:

   _I_ _n_ _d_ _e_ _p_ _e_ _n_ _d_ _e_ (_c_) _e_   _D_ _a_ _y_

2. Your child finishes high school:

   _ (_) _ _ _ _ (_) _   _ _ _ _

3. Children wear costumes:

   _ _ (_) _ _ _ _ _ _

4. A woman wears a beautiful white dress:

   _ (_) _ _ _ _ _

5. People bring gifts for a new baby:

   (_) _ _ _   _ _ _ (_) _

6. December 31:

   (_) _ _   _ _ _ _ _ _   _ _ _

7. Your friend is one year older:

   _ (_) _ _ _ _ _ _

8. February 14:

   _ _ _ _ _ (_) _ _ _ _ _   _ _ _

9. Your sister has a party in her new apartment:

   _ _ _ _ _ (_) _ _ _ _ _ _

B Write the circled letters from Exercise A.

   _c_ _ _ _ _ _ _ _ _ _ _

Write. Unscramble the letters to answer the question.

What's another word for a party?

   _c_ _ _ _ _ _ _ _ _ _ _

3 Wrap up

Complete the **Self-assessment** on page 145.

Review

1 Listening

Read the questions. Then listen and circle the answers.

1. Why is Ramona going to have a party?
   a. to celebrate her birthday
   b. (to celebrate her new apartment)

2. When is Ramona's party?
   a. next month
   b. next week

3. What does Ramona need?
   a. a painter
   b. a plumber

4. How many good painters does Fabio know?
   a. one
   b. two

5. Which painter does Fabio recommend?
   a. the first one
   b. the second one

6. What is the name of the second painter?
   a. Fabio
   b. Walter

Talk with a partner. Ask and answer the questions. Use complete sentences.

2 Grammar

A Write. Complete the conversation.

Rita Saba, could you ____*help*____ me with something? My teacher is going to
        1. help / helping

        retire tomorrow, and I want to buy a gift _____ her. What should I get?
                                                 2. to / for

Saba Let's see. Would she _____ some flowers?
                              3. like / likes

Rita Yes, she _____ . She loves flowers. Where can I buy them?
                  4. will / would

Saba There's a small flower shop downtown, and a bigger one near the school.

Rita _____ shop do you recommend?
         5. Which / Where

Saba I _____ the one near the school. It's cheaper.
           6. like / likes

B Write. Look at the answers. Write the questions.

1. **A** What _does Rita want to buy her teacher_ ?
   B Rita wants to buy her teacher a gift.

2. **A** What _____ ?
   B Her teacher would like some flowers.

3. **A** Which _____ ?
   B Saba recommends the flower shop near the school.

4. **A** Which _____ ?
   B The flower shop near the school is cheaper.

Talk with a partner. Ask and answer the questions.

3 Pronunciation: reduced forms

A Listen to the reduced forms of *Could you* and *Would you* in these sentences.

Could you
Could you help me?
Could you paint the wall, please?

Would you
Would you like some water?
Would you repair the refrigerator, please?

B Listen and repeat.

Could you
Could you send someone to help?
Could you recommend a painter?
Could you please fix this?

Would you
Would you turn on the light, please?
Would you unclog the sink?
Would you like a piece of cake?

C Listen to the sentences. Check (✓) the correct column.

	Could you	Would you
1.	☐	☐
2.	☐	☐
3.	☐	☐
4.	☐	☐
5.	☐	☐
6.	☐	☐

D Write four questions from Units 9 and 10. Find questions that begin with *Would you* or *Could you*.

1.
2.
3.
4.

Talk with a partner. Read the questions.

Projects

Online clothing store

A Use the Internet.

Find an online clothing store.

Keywords | women's clothes | men's clothes | children's clothes

B Make a chart.

Write the names of three people.
Find a gift of clothing for each person.
Write the item and the price.
Print a picture of each item.

Person	Gift	Price
my neighbor Ana	women's gray V-neck sweater	$39.95
my brother Paul	men's striped shirt	$44.50
my daughter Rachel	children's green and yellow dress	$29.99

C Share your information.

Show the pictures.
Talk about the gifts.
Talk about the online clothing stores.
What are the class's favorite store and gift?

Jobs and education

A Make a list.

What job do you want to have in five years?
Write three ideas.

1. hotel manager
2. nurse
3. receptionist

B Talk to people in your school.

Ask about the jobs on your list.
What education or training do you need?
Make a chart with the information.

C Share your information.

Make a class wall chart.
Talk about the jobs and training.

Job	Education or Training
hotel manager	associate's or bachelor's degree from a college or a degree from a hotel-management school
nurse	associate's or bachelor's degree in nursing
receptionist	high school diploma or GED

Weekend activities

A Use the Internet.

Find information about weekend activities in your city.

Find an activity for children, for parents, and for your friends.

If possible, print pictures of the activities.

Keywords (your city), weekend activities

B Take notes. Answer these questions.

1. Who is it for?
2. What kind of place is it?
3. What is the activity?
4. How much does it cost?

For	Place	Activity	Cost
children	pool	go swimming	$5
parents	beach	take a walk	$0
friends	park	play soccer	$0

C Share your information.

Tell your classmates about the places and activities.

Show the pictures.

Make a class wall chart of weekend activities.

Your medicine cabinet

A Choose a medicine.

What's in your medicine cabinet? Find a medicine.

B Answer these questions.

1. What is the name of the medicine?
2. Is this medicine for adults, for children, or for both?
3. Why should you take this medicine?
4. How much should an adult take at one time?
5. How often should you take this medicine?

1. What is the name of the medicine?

No More Pain.

2. Is this medicine for adults, for children, or for both?

For both.

C Share your information.

Draw a picture of this medicine, or cut out a picture of it from a magazine.

Paste the picture on a piece of paper.

Write the information about it.

Make a class booklet.

Projects

Take a trip

A Choose a city to visit.

Write the name of the city.

B Use the Internet.

Look for train and bus companies near you.

Keywords | Train schedule (your city) | Bus schedule (your city)

Read the schedules.
How often do the trains leave and return?
How often do the buses leave and return?

C Make a chart.

Write the information about your trip.

D Share your information.

Show your chart to your classmates.
Talk about the different schedules.

	Date and departure times	Date and return times
Chicago to Detroit by train	May 29 8:30 a.m. 2:30 p.m. 4:00 p.m.	June 1 9:30 a.m. 3:30 p.m. 5:00 p.m.
Chicago to Detroit by bus	May 29 8:00 a.m. 12:30 p.m.	June 1 10:00 a.m. 2:30 p.m.

Life events

A Think about important life events.
Write questions.

When were you born?

Where were you born?

B Interview a friend or relative.

Use the questions you wrote.
Write down the answers.

C Make a time line.

Include the important events.

1976	1994	1998	2000	2003
born in Mexico	first job	got married	came to the U.S.	first child

D Share your information.
Show your time line to
your classmates. Talk about the person you interviewed.

Furniture in a house

A Choose a room in a house.

Make a list of furniture for that room.

<u>living room</u>
sofa
recliner
coffee table
bookcase

B Look in magazines, catalogs, and online.

Find pictures of furniture.
Cut out or print the pictures.

C Make a picture of the room.

Draw the room. Put the furniture pictures
in the room.

D Share your information.

Show your room to your classmates.
Select your favorite rooms.
Put them together to make a house.

Job application

A Check (✓) a job that you would like.

☐ auto mechanic	☐ construction worker	☐ gas station attendant
☐ busboy	☐ cook	☐ nurse
☐ cashier	☐ dental assistant	☐ orderly

B Use the Internet.

Find a sample job application.

Keywords | sample job applications | | job application samples |

Print out an application.
Fill it out.
Use the job you checked.

C Share your information.

Share your job application with your classmates.

Projects

Home repairs

A Make a chart.

What are some problems in your home?
What kind of repair person do you need?

Problem	Repair person
cracked paint	painter
broken door	carpenter
leaking toilet	plumber

B Talk to your neighbors, relatives, and friends.

Write the names and phone numbers of repair people they recommend.

Manuel Maldonado / Painter
310-555-1234

C Share your information.

Talk about the repair people.
Make a class directory.

Holidays and celebrations

A Make groups.

Form 12 groups – one group for each month of the year.

B Use the Internet.

Find the dates of holidays and celebrations for your group.

Keywords
U.S. holidays
U.S. celebrations

international holidays
international celebrations

C Make a chart for your month.

D Share your information.

Show your chart to your classmates.
Make a poster of the holidays, celebrations, and dates for this year.

Month: January		
U.S. holidays and celebrations		
January 1	New Year's Day	
third Monday	Martin Luther King Jr. Day	
January	National Tea Month	
International holidays and celebrations		
January 1–3	Japanese New Year	Japan
January 6	Three Kings Day	Latin America
second Saturday	Children's Day	Thailand

Unit 1 Personal information

A Vocabulary Check (✓) the words you know.

- ☐ checked
- ☐ curly
- ☐ dress
- ☐ long
- ☐ pants
- ☐ plaid
- ☐ shirt
- ☐ short
- ☐ skirt
- ☐ small
- ☐ striped
- ☐ uniform

B Skills and functions Read the sentences. Check (✓) what you know.

I can use adjectives in the correct order: *She's wearing a **black striped** shirt.*		I can look for key words to answer reading questions.	
I can ask and answer questions using the present continuous: *What **are you doing** right now? **I'm reading**.*		I can write a paragraph describing a person.	
I can ask and answer questions using the simple present: *What **does** he **do** every Saturday? He always **watches** TV.*		I can understand an order form.	

C What's next? Choose one.

☐ I am ready for the unit test.   ☐ I need more practice with _____ .

Unit 2 At school

A Vocabulary Check (✓) the words you know.

- ☐ accounting
- ☐ automotive repair
- ☐ computer lab
- ☐ culinary arts
- ☐ goal
- ☐ hotel management
- ☐ keyboard
- ☐ lab instructor
- ☐ landscape design
- ☐ nursing
- ☐ open a business
- ☐ vocational course

B Skills and functions Read the sentences. Check (✓) what you know.

I can ask and answer questions using **want** and **need**: *What **do** they **want** to do? What **do** you **need** to do?*		I can read quickly to get the main idea.	
I can give advice about how to reach goals.		I can write about my goals.	
I can talk about the future using *will*: *What **will** she **do** on Tuesday? She'**ll go** to work.*		I can understand a course catalog.	

C What's next? Choose one.

☐ I am ready for the unit test.   ☐ I need more practice with _____ .

Unit 3 Friends and family

A Vocabulary Check (✓) the words you know.

☐ broke down	☐ do the laundry	☐ get up	☐ make the bed
☐ buy groceries	☐ fix the engine	☐ have a cell phone	☐ take a bath
☐ do the dishes	☐ get dressed	☐ make lunch	☐ take a nap

B Skills and functions Read the sentences. Check (✓) what you know.

I can ask and answer questions using the simple past with regular and irregular verbs: *What **did** they **do** last night? They **went** to the movies and **listened** to music.*		I can ask and answer questions about daily activities.	
I can decide when to use the simple present and when to use the simple past: *We usually **eat** dinner at 8:00. Yesterday, we **ate** dinner at 6:30.*		When I read, I can look for words that tell the order things happened.	
I can write a journal entry about my day.		I can understand cell phone calling plans.	

C What's next? Choose one.

☐ I am ready for the unit test.   ☐ I need more practice with _____ .

Unit 4 Health

A Vocabulary Check (✓) the words you know.

☐ accident	☐ crutches	☐ prescription	☐ take medicine
☐ allergies	☐ hurt	☐ stiff neck	☐ warning label
☐ chills	☐ injury	☐ swollen knee	☐ X-ray

B Skills and functions Read the sentences. Check (✓) what you know.

I can ask and answer questions using **have to**: *What **does** she **have to** do? She **has to** take her medicine.*		I can read a warning label.	
I can ask and answer questions using **should**: *What **should** they do? They **should** stay in the shade.*		I can complete an accident report form.	
I can talk about health problems.		I can understand a medicine label.	

C What's next? Choose one.

☐ I am ready for the unit test.   ☐ I need more practice with _____ .

Unit 5 Around town

A Vocabulary Check (✓) the words you know.

☐ buy souvenirs	☐ never	☐ stay with relatives	☐ ticket booth
☐ go sightseeing	☐ rarely	☐ suitcase	☐ waiting room
☐ information desk	☐ sometimes	☐ take pictures	☐ write postcards

B Skills and functions Read the sentences. Check (✓) what you know.

I can ask and answer questions using *How often* and *How long*: *How often does the train leave? Every 30 minutes.* *How long does it take? About three hours.*		I can use adverbs of frequency: *He rarely rides his bike. She always takes a taxi.*	
I can read a bus schedule.		I can write a letter to a friend about a trip.	
I can talk about travel activities.		I can understand a train schedule.	

C What's next? Choose one.

☐ I am ready for the unit test.   ☐ I need more practice with _____ .

Unit 6 Time

A Vocabulary Check (✓) the words you know.

☐ become a citizen	☐ find a job	☐ graduate	☐ move
☐ citizenship exam	☐ get married	☐ have a baby	☐ photo album
☐ fall in love	☐ get promoted	☐ immigrate	☐ retired

B Skills and functions Read the sentences. Check (✓) what you know.

I can ask and answer *When* questions to talk about the simple past: *When did you get married? I got married in 1980.*		I can write a paragraph about important events in my life.	
I can use time phrases: *three weeks ago, on Sunday, at 4:00 p.m., last year.*		I can understand an application for a marriage license.	
I can talk about life events.		I can make a time line.	

C What's next? Choose one.

☐ I am ready for the unit test.   ☐ I need more practice with _____ .

Unit 7 Shopping

A Vocabulary Check (✓) the words you know.

- ☐ appliances
- ☐ cheap
- ☐ comfortable
- ☐ customer
- ☐ expensive
- ☐ furniture
- ☐ gift
- ☐ heavy
- ☐ lamp
- ☐ piano
- ☐ price tag
- ☐ sofa

B Skills and functions Read the sentences. Check (✓) what you know.

I can use comparatives: *bigger, cheaper, heavier, more expensive*.		I can read a newspaper article.	
I can use superlatives: *the biggest, the cheapest, the heaviest, the most expensive*.		I can write about the best gift I ever received.	
I can talk about furniture.		I can understand a sales receipt.	

C What's next? Choose one.

☐ I am ready for the unit test.   ☐ I need more practice with _____ .

Unit 8 Work

A Vocabulary Check (✓) the words you know.

- ☐ clear tables
- ☐ co-worker
- ☐ deliver
- ☐ handle money
- ☐ job duties
- ☐ lab
- ☐ linens
- ☐ orderly
- ☐ patient
- ☐ pick up
- ☐ prepare
- ☐ supplies

B Skills and functions Read the sentences. Check (✓) what you know.

I can ask and answer **Where** and **What** questions in the simple past: **What did** he **do? Where did** you **go?**		I can read and understand a letter of recommendation.	
I can use the conjunctions **and**, **or**, and **but**: *She went to work **and** took notes.*		I can scan a text for specific information (names, dates).	
I can write about my employment history.		I can understand a weekly time sheet.	

C What's next? Choose one.

☐ I am ready for the unit test.   ☐ I need more practice with _____ .

Unit 9 Daily living

A Vocabulary Check (✓) the words you know.

- ☐ clogged
- ☐ electrician
- ☐ fix
- ☐ garbage
- ☐ jammed
- ☐ a leak
- ☐ lightbulb
- ☐ plumber
- ☐ repair
- ☐ a sink
- ☐ tenant
- ☐ unclog

B Skills and functions Read the sentences. Check (✓) what you know.

I can ask *Which* questions using the simple present: *Which electrician do you recommend?*		I can talk about problems in a home or an apartment.	
I can make requests using *Can*, *Could*, *Will*, and *Would*: *Could you clean the bathroom, please?*		I can write a letter of complaint to a building manager or landlord.	
I can read a notice to tenants.		I can understand an invoice.	

C What's next? Choose one.

☐ I am ready for the unit test.   ☐ I need more practice with _____ .

Unit 10 Leisure

A Vocabulary Check (✓) the words you know.

- ☐ balloons
- ☐ cake
- ☐ card
- ☐ celebrate
- ☐ flowers
- ☐ a gift
- ☐ graduation party
- ☐ housewarming
- ☐ invitation
- ☐ a present
- ☐ thank-you note
- ☐ wedding

B Skills and functions Read the sentences. Check (✓) what you know.

I can ask and answer questions with *Would you like . . . ?*: *Would you like a cup of coffee? Yes, I would.*		I can look for examples of the main idea in a paragraph.	
I can make statements with direct and indirect objects: *I gave her some books*.		I can read and write a thank-you note.	
I can talk about celebrations.		I can understand an invitation to a party.	

C What's next? Choose one.

☐ I am ready for the unit test.   ☐ I need more practice with _____ .

Reference

Present continuous

| Affirmative statements

What	am	I	doing now?

I'm	working.

What	is is is	he she it	doing now?

He's She's It's	working.

What	are are are	we you they	doing now?

We're You're They're	working.

I'm	=	I am		We're	=	We are
He's	=	He is		You're	=	You are
She's	=	She is		They're	=	They are
It's	=	It is				

Simple present

Wh- questions: What | Affirmative statements

What	do	I you we they	do every day?

I You We They	usually	work.

What	does	he she it	do every day?

He She It	usually	works.

Wh- questions: When | Affirmative statements

When	do	I you we they	usually work?

I You We They	usually	work	on Friday.

When	does	he she it	usually work?

He She It	usually	works	on Friday.

Simple present of *need* and *want*

What	do	I you we they	want to do? need to do?
What	does	he she it	want to do? need to do?

Affirmative statements

I You We They	want need	to go.
He She It	wants needs	to go.

Simple present of *have to* + verb

Wh- questions: What

What	do	I you we they	have to do?
What	does	he she it	have to do?

Affirmative statements

I You We They	have to	go.
He She It	has to	go.

Simple present with *Which* questions

Wh- questions: Which

Which one	do	I you we they	recommend?
Which one	does	he she it	recommend?

Affirmative statements

I You We They	recommend	Joe's Repair Shop.
He She It	recommends	Joe's Repair Shop.

Simple past with regular and irregular verbs

Wh- questions: What

What	did	I you he she it we you they	do?

Affirmative statements

I You He She It We You They	stayed. ate.

Negative statements

I You He She It We You They	didn't	stay. eat.

didn't = did not

Yes / No questions

Did	I you he she it we you they	stay? eat?

Short answers

Yes,	I you he she it we you they	did.	No,	I you he she it we you they	didn't.

Wh- questions: When

When	did	I you he she it we you they	move? leave?

Affirmative statements

I You He She It We You They	moved left	in July. last week.

Wh- questions: Where

Where	did	I you he she it we you they	go?

Affirmative statements

I You He She It We You They	stayed went	home.

Future with *will*

Wh- questions: *What*

What	will	I you he she it we you they	do	tomorrow?

Affirmative statements

I'll You'll He'll She'll It'll We'll You'll They'll	probably	work.

'll = will

Negative statements

I You He She It We You They	won't	work.

won't = will not

Should

Wh- questions: *What*

What	should	I you he she it we you they	do?

Affirmative statements

I You He She It We You They	should	work.

Negative statements

I You He She It We You They	shouldn't	work.

shouldn't = should not

Would you like . . . ?

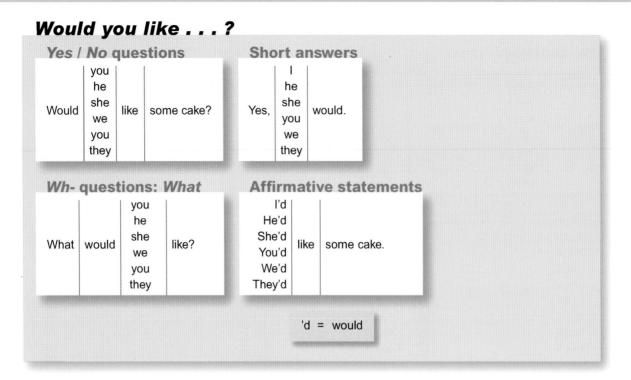

Yes / No questions

Would	you he she we you they	like	some cake?

Short answers

Yes,	I he she you we they	would.

Wh- questions: *What*

What	would	you he she we you they	like?

Affirmative statements

I'd He'd She'd You'd We'd They'd	like	some cake.

'd = would

Direct and indirect objects

Tim gave a present to	Mary. me. you. him. her. it. us. you. them.

Tim gave	Mary me you him her it us you them	a present.

Comparative and superlative adjectives

	Adjective	Comparative	Superlative
Adjectives with one syllable	cheap	cheaper	the cheapest
	large	larger	the largest
	long	longer	the longest
	new	newer	the newest
	nice	nicer	the nicest
	old	older	the oldest
	short	shorter	the shortest
	small	smaller	the smallest
	tall	taller	the tallest
	young	younger	the youngest
Adjectives with one syllable ending in a vowel-consonant pair	big	bigger	the biggest
	fat	fatter	the fattest
	hot	hotter	the hottest
	sad	sadder	the saddest
Adjectives with two or more syllables	beautiful	more beautiful	the most beautiful
	comfortable	more comfortable	the most comfortable
	crowded	more crowded	the most crowded
	expensive	more expensive	the most expensive
Adjectives ending in -y	friendly	friendlier	the friendliest
	heavy	heavier	the heaviest
	pretty	prettier	the prettiest
Irregular adjectives	good	better	the best
	bad	worse	the worst

Past tense irregular verbs

be	→ was/were	eat	→ ate	know	→ knew	sit	→ sat
become	→ became	fall	→ fell	leave	→ left	sleep	→ slept
begin	→ began	feel	→ felt	lose	→ lost	speak	→ spoke
break	→ broke	fight	→ fought	make	→ made	spend	→ spent
bring	→ brought	find	→ found	meet	→ met	stand	→ stood
build	→ built	fly	→ flew	pay	→ paid	steal	→ stole
buy	→ bought	forget	→ forgot	put	→ put	swim	→ swam
catch	→ caught	give	→ gave	read	→ read	take	→ took
choose	→ chose	go	→ went	ride	→ rode	teach	→ taught
come	→ came	have	→ had	run	→ ran	tell	→ told
cost	→ cost	hear	→ heard	say	→ said	think	→ thought
cut	→ cut	hide	→ hid	see	→ saw	understand	→ understood
do	→ did	hold	→ held	sell	→ sold	wake	→ woke
drink	→ drank	hurt	→ hurt	send	→ sent	wear	→ wore
drive	→ drove	keep	→ kept	sing	→ sang	write	→ wrote

Ordinal numbers

1st first	9th ninth	17th seventeenth	25th twenty-fifth
2nd second	10th tenth	18th eighteenth	26th twenty-sixth
3rd third	11th eleventh	19th nineteenth	27th twenty-seventh
4th fourth	12th twelfth	20th twentieth	28th twenty-eighth
5th fifth	13th thirteenth	21st twenty-first	29th twenty-ninth
6th sixth	14th fourteenth	22nd twenty-second	30th thirtieth
7th seventh	15th fifteenth	23rd twenty-third	31st thirty-first
8th eighth	16th sixteenth	24th twenty-fourth	

Metric equivalents

1 inch = 25 millimeters	1 dry ounce = 28 grams	1 fluid ounce = 30 milliliters
1 foot = 30 centimeters	1 pound = .45 kilograms	1 quart = .95 liters
1 yard = .9 meters	1 mile = 1.6 kilometers	1 gallon = 3.8 liters

Converting Fahrenheit temperatures to Celsius

Subtract 30 and divide by 2: $80°F$ = approximately $25°C$

Spelling rules

Comparative adjectives

- For adjectives with one syllable, add -er or -r:
  old → older   nice → nicer
- For adjectives with one syllable ending in a vowel-consonant pair, double the consonant and add -er:
  big → bigger
- For adjectives with two or more syllables, add *more*:
  expensive → more expensive
- For adjectives ending in -y, change *y* to *i* and add -er:
  pretty → prettier

Superlative adjectives

- For adjectives with one syllable, add *the* before the adjective and add -est or -st:
  old → the oldest   nice → the nicest
- For adjectives with one syllable ending in a vowel-consonant pair, add *the*, double the consonant, and add -est:
  big → the biggest
- For adjectives with two or more syllables, add *the most*:
  expensive → the most expensive
- For adjectives ending in -y, add *the*, change *y* to *i*, and add -est:
  pretty → the prettiest

Punctuation rules

- Sentences can end with a period (.), question mark (?), or exclamation point (!):
  Simple statement: *We have cookies.*
  Question: *Do we have cookies?*
  Strong feeling: *We have cookies!*
- Put a comma after every item when a list has three or more items:
  We have soda, coffee, and water.
- Use a comma after time phrases like *After class, On the weekend, In 2001,* or *On July 4th* when they come at the beginning of a sentence.
- Use a comma after sequence words:
  First, I washed the dirty clothes.
- Begin a new paragraph when you start a new topic or change the tense.
- Paragraphs start with an indent.
- Indent the paragraphs in an informal note. Don't indent the date or *Dear ____* .

Welcome

Page 3, Exercise 2A – Track 2

1. A What's your name?
   B Ben Navarro.
2. A How do you spell your last name?
   B N-A-V-A-R-R-O.
3. A Do you have a middle initial?
   B Yes. It's J.
4. A What's your address?
   B 1737 Van Dam Street, Brooklyn, New York.
5. A What's your zip code?
   B It's 11222.
6. A Do you have an apartment number?
   B Yes. It's 3A.
7. A What's your home phone number?
   B 718-555-5983.
8. A What's your date of birth?
   B January 18th, 1982.

Page 4, Exercise 3A – Track 3

1. Armin and Stefan do their homework and study in the library every day.
2. Yesterday they wrote paragraphs about their families.
3. Right now they're studying for a vocabulary test.
4. Tomorrow they're not going to study in the library.
5. Stefan is going to go to work tomorrow afternoon, and Armin is going to take his grandmother to the doctor.

Page 4, Exercise 3B – Track 4

Right now it's 11:30 p.m., but Stefan isn't sleeping. He's studying for an English test.

Stefan goes to school every morning from 9 o'clock to 12 o'clock. After class, he usually meets Armin in the library, and they study together.

Yesterday was different. Stefan didn't go to the library. He went to work. He worked from 2:00 p.m. until 10:00 p.m. Then he came home and started studying. He studied until 2 o'clock in the morning.

Tomorrow Stefan is going to be very tired!

Page 5, Exercise 4A – Track 5

A Hi. I'm looking for a job.
B What can you do?
A I can use a computer very well. I can speak English and Korean. I can help students with their homework, and I can read to children.
B Can you write in English?
A Yes, I can.
B Can you speak Spanish?
A No, I can't. But I'm going to learn.

Unit 1: Personal information

Lesson A: Get ready

Page 7, Exercises 2A and 2B – Track 6

Conversation A

A Shoko, who's this?
B This is a picture of my daughter, Victoria.
A What's she wearing?
B Her soccer uniform. She plays every day. She's very athletic.
A Wow. She's really tall.
B Yes, she is. She looks like her father.
A She's a pretty girl. Her long black hair is beautiful.

Conversation B

A Shoko, is that your son?
B Yes. This is my teenage son, Eddie.
A What's he doing?
B He's playing computer games. He always plays computer games!
A Does he have a lot of friends?
B No, not many. He's a very quiet boy.

Conversation C

A This is a picture of my husband, Mark.
B Oh, Shoko, he *is* tall!
A Yes, he is. He wears very large shirts and pants. I buy his clothes at a special store.
B What does he do?
A He's an engineer. He's very smart. He studies English, too.
B You have a really nice family.
A Thanks.

Lesson D: Reading

Page 12, Exercise 2 – Track 7

Hi Karin,

How are you doing? Guess what! Today is my daughter's birthday. The last time you saw Victoria, she was three years old. Now she's 17! She's tall and very athletic. She likes sports. She plays soccer every afternoon. Here is her photo. She's wearing her red and white striped soccer uniform. She usually wears jeans and a T-shirt. Victoria is also a very good student. She has lots of friends and goes with them to the mall every weekend. How are your daughters? Please send a photo!
Let's stay in touch.
Shoko

Page 13, Exercise 4A – Track 8

1. a hat
2. a tie
3. a watch
4. a scarf
5. gloves
6. a purse
7. earrings
8. a necklace
9. a bracelet
10. a ring

Unit 2: At school

Lesson A: Get ready
Page 19, Exercises 2A and 2B – Track 9

Conversation A

A Oh, what's wrong with this computer?!

B Um, Joseph, do you need help?

A Oh, thanks, Eva. I'm having trouble with this keyboard. I need to take a computer class.

B Ask the teacher about keyboarding classes. She helped me find a citizenship class.

A That's a great idea. I'll talk to Mrs. Lee after class. Thanks!

B You're welcome, Joseph. Good luck!

Conversation B

A Oh, hi, Joseph. Do you need something?

B Yes, Mrs. Lee. I want to learn keyboarding skills. What do I need to do?

A Hmm . . . keyboarding skills. Do you need to use a computer at work?

B No, not right now. But someday I want to open my own business. I'm pretty sure I'll need to use a computer then.

A Well, you can study keyboarding in the computer lab across the hall. You could talk with Mr. Stephens. He's the lab instructor.

B Thanks, Mrs. Lee. I'll talk to Mr. Stephens right now.

Conversation C

A Hello, Mr. Stephens. My name is Joseph. Mrs. Lee told me to come here. I want to learn keyboarding.

B That's great. You can join my keyboarding class. First you need to register with Mrs.

Smith in the Registration Office.

A Great. I'll go register now.

B But there's one problem.

A One problem?

B Yes. The Registration Office is closed today. You can register next week.

A OK. Thanks.

Lesson D: Reading
Page 24, Exercise 2 – Track 10

What are your future goals? What steps do you need to take? I want to open my own electronics store. I need to take three steps to reach my goal. First, I need to learn keyboarding. Second, I need to take business classes. Third, I need to work in an electronics store. I will probably open my store in a couple of years.

Page 25, Exercise 4A – Track 11

1. automotive repair
2. computer technology
3. accounting
4. nursing
5. counseling
6. hotel management
7. culinary arts
8. home health care
9. landscape design

Unit 3: Friends and family

Lesson A: Get ready
Page 33, Exercises 2A and 2B – Track 12

Conversation A

A Rigatoni Restaurant. Daniel speaking.

B Hi, Daniel? It's me.

A Rosa? Hi. Is everything OK?

B Not really. I went to the supermarket with the children, and the car broke down.

A The car broke down! What's wrong?

B I don't know. I think it's the engine.

A Did you open the hood?

B Yes, I did. There's a lot of smoke!

A Where are you?

B I'm at the side of the road near the supermarket.

A Stay there. I'm going to leave work right now. I'll be there in ten minutes.

B OK. I have a lot of groceries in the trunk. Please hurry.

Conversation B

A Mike's Auto Repair.

B Hi, Mike, it's Rosa – Daniel's wife?

A Oh, hi, Rosa. How are you?

B Well, not so good.

A Why? What's wrong?

B Well, this morning I went to the store to buy groceries for a picnic, but then our car broke down. My husband came and picked us up.

A Oh, I'm sorry, Rosa.

B Could you pick up the car for us? It's on the side of the road near the supermarket.

A Of course. I'll pick it up and take it to my shop this afternoon.

B Thanks, Mike.

Conversation C

A Hello, Swift Dry Cleaner's.

B Hi, Ling. It's Rosa. How are you?

A I'm good. I'm almost done with work. Will I see you tonight?

B I'm not sure. We had car trouble today. I need a ride to school tonight. Can you pick me up?

A Sure. What time?

B I usually leave my house at 7 o'clock.

A OK. I'll pick you up at seven.

B That's great. You're a good friend, Ling. Thank you.

A No problem. See you tonight.

Lesson D: Reading

Page 38, Exercise 2 – Track 13

Thursday, June 20th

Today was a bad day! On Thursday, my children and I usually go to the park for a picnic, but today we had a problem. We drove to the store to buy groceries, and then the car broke down. I checked the engine, and there was a lot of smoke. Luckily, I had my cell phone! First, I called my husband at work. He left early, picked us up, and took us home. Next, I called the mechanic. Finally, I called Ling and asked for a ride to school tonight. In the end, we didn't go to the park because it was too late. Instead, we had a picnic in our backyard. Then, Ling drove me to school.

Page 39, Exercise 4A – Track 14

1. make lunch
2. take a bath
3. do the dishes
4. do the laundry
5. get up
6. do homework
7. take a nap
8. make the bed
9. get dressed

Unit 4: Health

Lesson A: Get ready

Page 45, Exercises 2A and 2B – Track 15

Conversation A

A Hello?
B Lily, it's me. I had a little accident.
A Are you OK, Hamid? What happened?
B I fell off a ladder at work. I hurt my leg.
A Hamid, you should go to the hospital!
B I'm at the hospital now. But listen, you have to pick up the children at school. I have to wait for the doctor.
A OK, I'll pick up the children. I'll see you back at home.
B OK, thanks, Lily. Bye.

Conversation B

A Hello?
B Chris, it's Hamid.
A Hey, how's it going?
B Not so good. I had a little accident at work. I fell off a ladder.
A Oh, no. Are you OK?
B Well, I hurt my leg. I'm at the hospital now, and I had to get an X-ray. Could you come to the hospital and drive me home?
A Of course. What's the address?
B It's 3560 East 54th Street. You should take the highway.
A OK. I'm leaving right now.
B Thanks, Chris. Bye.

Conversation C

A Ace Construction.
B Hi, Angie. It's Hamid. I need to talk to Mr. Jackson, please.
A Hi, Hamid. Just a second.
C Hi, Hamid. Jackson here. How's it going? Did you finish painting the house on Main Street?
B Well, no. I had a little accident. I slipped and fell off the ladder. I'm at the hospital now.
C Oh, no! Are you badly hurt?
B I don't know. I had to get an X-ray of my leg. The doctor is looking at the X-ray now.
C Hamid, you have to fill out an accident report. Call me after you see the doctor.
B OK. What about the paint job?
C Don't worry. Felipe will finish it. Stay home tomorrow. You should rest.
B OK. Thanks, Mr. Jackson. Bye.

Lesson D: Reading

Page 50, Exercise 2 – Track 16

Warning: Prevent accidents. Read before using!
• Face the ladder when climbing up and down.
• Don't carry a lot of equipment while climbing a ladder – wear a tool belt.
• Never stand on the shelf of the ladder – stand on the steps.
• Never stand on the top step of a ladder.
• Be safe! Always read and follow the safety stickers.

Page 51, Exercise 4A – Track 17

1. chills
2. a sprained wrist
3. chest pains
4. high blood pressure
5. allergies
6. a swollen knee
7. a bad cut
8. a rash
9. a stiff neck

Unit 5: Around town

Lesson A: Get ready

Page 59, Exercises 2A and 2B – Track 18

Conversation A

A Attention, please. This is an announcement.
B What's that, Binh?
C That's just an announcement, Mom. The announcer is giving train information. We should listen.
A Trains to Washington, D.C., leave every hour. The next train to Washington, D.C., will leave at 7:20 from Track 1. I repeat. The next train to Washington, D.C., will leave at 7:20 from Track 1.
B That was about trains to Washington. We need information about trains to New York.

C Wait. Here's another announcement.

A Trains to New York City leave every — — . The next train to New York will leave at — — . I repeat. The next train to New York will leave at — — from Track 2.

B Oh, no! We didn't hear the information about New York!

Conversation B

A There's an information desk over there. You can ask about trains from Philadelphia to New York.

B Oh, good. . . . Excuse me. I need some train information.

C How can I help you?

B I'm taking my mother to New York City today. How often do trains go to New York?

C Trains leave for New York every 30 minutes.

B When does the next train leave for New York?

C The 7:05 train just left. The next train leaves at 7:35 from Track 3.

B Thanks.

C Do you have tickets? You can get them at the ticket booth over there.

B No, we don't have tickets. Thank you very much.

Conversation C

A I got our tickets, Mom. Our train leaves in 25 minutes.

B Good. We don't have to wait long.

A Do you want to sit down? We can sit in the waiting area.

B That's a good idea. My suitcase is heavy. . . . This train station is beautiful.

A Yeah, it really is. I always travel by train. It's a lot easier than driving.

B How long does it take to drive to New York?

A It usually takes about 2 hours to drive. It takes less than one and a half hours by train.

C Attention, please. The train to New York is now boarding on Track 3.

A That's our train, Mom. Let's go!

Lesson D: Reading

Page 64, Exercise 2 – Track 19

Dear Layla,

Right now, my mother is visiting me here in Philadelphia. I rarely see her because she comes to Philadelphia only once a year. She usually stays for one month. Here is a photo of my mother at the airport last week. She was happy to see me!

This year, I want to take my mother to New York City. I want to show her the Statue of Liberty and Central Park. It takes about one and a half hours to get to New York by train. We are excited about our trip. Can you meet us there? Let me know.

Your friend,
Binh

Page 65, Exercise 4A – Track 20

1. go shopping
2. stay at a hotel
3. take a suitcase
4. buy souvenirs
5. go swimming
6. stay with relatives
7. take pictures
8. write postcards
9. go sightseeing

Unit 6: Time

Lesson A: Get ready

Page 71, Exercises 2A and 2B – Track 21

Conversation A

A Olga, I love your new apartment.

B Thanks, Victoria. We moved in two months ago. You're our first visitor.

A Is that your wedding picture?

B Yes, it is. That's my husband and me a long time ago.

A What a good-looking bride and groom! When did you get married?

B Let's see. We got married in 1983.

A You were young! My husband and I had our third wedding anniversary last month. Do you have more pictures?

B Sure. They're in our photo album. Do you want to see them?

A I'd love to.

Conversation B

A Your pictures are wonderful. You have a lovely family.

B Thanks!

A How old are your children?

B My son, Sergey, is 19 now. His birthday was three days ago. He started college in September.

A When did your daughter start college?

B Start college! Natalya's only 14!

A Wow. She's tall for her age.

B Yes, she is. She started high school on Tuesday.

Conversation C

A Is that a picture of Russia?

B Yes. That's in Moscow.

A Did you live in Moscow?

B Yes. We met in Moscow. We went to school there before we got married.

A It looks like an interesting city.

B Oh, it is!

A When did you move to the United States?

B We moved here about 14 years ago.

A Were your children born here?

B Natalya was. Sergey was born in Russia, like us.

Lesson D: Reading

Page 76, Exercise 2 – Track 22

An Interesting Life

A What happened after you graduated from high school?

B I went to university in Moscow, and I met my husband there. It was a long time ago! We were in the same class. We fell in love and got married on April 2nd, 1983. We had a small wedding in Moscow.

A What happened after you got married?

B I finished university and found a job. I was a teacher. Then, I had a baby. My husband and I were very excited to have a little boy.

A When did you move to the United States?

B We immigrated about 14 years ago. We became American citizens ten years ago.

Page 77, Exercise 4A – Track 23

1. retired
2. started a business
3. had a baby
4. fell in love
5. got engaged
6. got married
7. got a divorce
8. immigrated
9. got promoted

Unit 7: Shopping

Lesson A: Get ready

Page 85, Exercises 2A and 2B – Track 24

Conversation A

A Good afternoon, folks. I'm Mike. How can I help you?

B Hi, I'm Denise. This is my husband, Nick. We need some furniture.

C A *lot* of furniture!

B We bought a house two days ago.

A Congratulations! This is the right place for furniture *and* appliances. We're having our biggest sale of the year. All our furniture is marked down 20 percent.

B Wow! 20 percent.

A We have chairs, lamps, sofas, . . . Look around. We have the best prices in town.

B Are the appliances 20 percent off, too?

A Yes! Refrigerators, stoves – everything in the store is 20 percent off.

C Thanks.

Conversation B

A Nick, look at that sofa. It's very pretty!

B Which one? The brown one?

A No, not the brown one, the blue one. It looks nice and comfortable. I like it.

B Hmm. But the brown sofa is bigger. I want a *big* sofa.

A Well, it *is* bigger, but look at the price, Nick. It's much more expensive than the blue sofa.

B Whoa! A thousand dollars? That's crazy!

A Look, there are some more sofas over there. Maybe they're cheaper.

B I sure hope so.

Conversation C

A Oh, look, Nick. They have pianos for sale.

B Pianos? But we aren't looking for a piano. We're looking for a sofa.

A I *love* this piano. Excuse me, miss? Do you work here?

C Yes. My name is Tara. How can I help you?

A Could you tell me about this piano?

C Oh, the upright piano? It's very old, but it's the most beautiful piano in the store. It also has a beautiful sound. Listen.

A Wow. Is it expensive?

C Well, it's $1,200. This small piano is cheaper, but the sound isn't the same.

A The upright piano is better. Let's buy it, Nick!

B Hey, not so fast! We came here to buy a sofa, not a piano!

Lesson D: Reading

Page 90, Exercise 2 – Track 25

Today's Question
What's the best thing you ever bought?

The best thing I ever bought was an old piano. I bought it in a used-furniture store last month. It was the most beautiful piano in the store, but it wasn't very expensive. It has a beautiful sound. Now my two children are taking piano lessons. I love to hear music in the house.
Denise Robinson – Charleston, South Carolina

I bought a used van five years ago. I used my van to help people move and to deliver stoves and refrigerators from a secondhand appliance store. I made a lot of money with that van. Now I have my own business. That van is the best thing I ever bought.
Sammy Chin – Myrtle Beach, South Carolina

Page 91, Exercise 4A – Track 26

1. end table
2. bookcase
3. dresser
4. entertainment center
5. sofa bed
6. mirror
7. china cabinet
8. coffee table
9. recliner

Unit 8: Work

Lesson A: Get ready

Page 97, Exercises 2A and 2B – Track 27

Conversation A

A Hey, Marco. How are you?

B Oh, hi, Arlen. I'm fine. I had a busy day today.

A What did you do?

B Hmm . . . let's see. This morning, I delivered flowers to patients and picked up X-rays from the lab. I also delivered clean linens to the third floor. This afternoon, I made the beds on the second floor and prepared the rooms. And now I'm delivering supplies.

A Wow. You *did* have a busy day!

Conversation B

A Hi, John. How's it going?

B Hi, Marco. I'm tired. I worked the night shift last night.

A Oh, no.

B I like this job, but I don't like the night shift.

A I like this job, too, but I don't like the pay. I'm thinking about going back to school.

B Really? School is expensive.

A I know. Maybe I can find a part-time job and go to school full-time.

B Maybe you can work here part-time. You should ask about it.

Conversation C

A Is this the HR Office? Human Resources?

B Yes, come on in. I'm Suzanne Briggs. I'm the HR Assistant.

A Hi, Suzanne. I'm Marco Alba. I'm an orderly here.

B Hi, Marco. Have a seat. How can I help you?

A I like my job here, but I don't want to be an orderly forever. I want to go to nursing school and become a nurse.

B A nurse? That's great, Marco!

A I want to go to nursing school full-time and work part-time.

B That's a great idea! A lot of employees do that.

A Can I work part-time here at Valley Hospital?

B I don't know. Can you come back tomorrow? I'll find out about part-time jobs for you.

A Sure. Thanks, Suzanne. See you tomorrow.

Lesson D: Reading

Page 102, Exercise 2 – Track 28

Dear Mr. O'Hara:

I am happy to write this letter of recommendation for Marco Alba. Marco started working at Valley Hospital as an orderly in 2003. He takes patients from their rooms to the lab, delivers X-rays, and takes flowers and mail to patients. He also delivers linens and supplies. He is an excellent worker, and his co-workers like him very much.

We are sorry to lose Marco. He wants to go to school and needs to work part-time, but we don't have a part-time job for him right now. I recommend Marco very highly. Please contact me for more information.

Sincerely,

Suzanne Briggs

Human Resources Assistant

Page 103, Exercise 4A – Track 29

1. repair cars
2. operate large machines
3. clear tables
4. prepare food
5. help the nurses
6. take care of a family
7. handle money
8. pump gas
9. assist the dentist

Unit 9: Daily living

Lesson A: Get ready

Page 111, Exercises 2A and 2B – Track 30

Conversation A

A Hello, Building Manager.

B Hi, this is Stella Taylor in Apartment 4B. I've got a problem. The washing machine overflowed. And the dishwasher's leaking, too. And the sink is clogged. Could you please recommend a plumber?

A Well, I usually use two different plumbers.

B Which one do you recommend?

A Let's see. His name is Don Brown. He has a company on Main Street. Here's the phone number: 555-4564. He's really good.

B Thanks. I'll call him right away.

Conversation B

A Brown's Plumbing Service, Martha speaking. May I help you?

B I hope so. My washing machine overflowed, and my dishwasher is leaking all over the floor, *and* my sink is clogged. May I speak to Don Brown, please?

A Oh, Don's out right now on a job. But he'll be finished in an hour. He can come then. Can you wait an hour?

B One hour? Hmm. I need to go to work soon. Maybe my neighbor can unlock the door for him. My address is 3914 Fifth Street, Apartment 4B.

A OK. He'll be there in an hour.

B Thank you.

Conversation C

A Russell Taylor speaking.

B Hi, Russell. It's me. I have bad news. The washing machine overflowed, and the dishwasher is leaking on the floor, *and* the sink is clogged!

A Oh, no. Look, I'm really busy at work right now. Could you please call a plumber?

B I already did.

A You did? Which plumber did you call?

B Brown's Plumbing Service. The plumber will be here in an hour.

A But you're going to work.

B It's OK. I asked Mrs. Lee to let him in.

A All right, Stella. I'll see you tonight.

Lesson D: Reading

Page 116, Exercise 2 – Track 31

Attention, tenants:

Do you have problems in your apartment? Is anyone fixing them?

• Many tenants have broken windows.

• Tenants on the third floor have no lights in the hall.

• A tenant on the second floor has a leaking ceiling.

• Tenants on the first floor smell garbage every day.

I'm really upset! We need to get together and write a letter of complaint to the manager of the building.

Come to a meeting Friday night at 7 p.m. in Apartment 4B.
Stella Taylor, Tenant 4B

Page 117, Exercise 4A – Track 32

1. broken
2. dripping
3. torn
4. scratched
5. bent
6. burned out
7. cracked
8. stained
9. jammed

Unit 10: Leisure

Lesson A: Get ready

Page 123, Exercises 2A and 2B – Track 33

Conversation A

A Aunt Ana! Hello!

B Hi, Celia. Congratulations on your graduation! This is a wonderful party!

A Thank you for coming. Would you like some cake? My mother made it.

B I'd love some. I'm starving.

A Would you like something to drink?

B No, thanks. Here. I brought you some flowers. They're from my garden.

A Red roses! They're beautiful! Thank you.

Conversation B

A Hello, Mrs. Campbell. Thank you for coming to my party.

B Celia, I'm so proud of you. You were my best student. You started English class three years ago, and now you have your GED! You worked very hard.

A Thank you, Mrs. Campbell. You helped me a lot.

B Here. I brought you a card.

A Oh, thank you! . . . Oh, that's so nice. Thank you, Mrs. Campbell.

B You're welcome.

A Come and join the party. Would you like a piece of cake?

B Yes, please. I'd love some.

Conversation C

A Hi, Sue. Thanks for coming. Where are your children?

B They're with my mother, so I can't stay long. I just wanted to congratulate you.

A Thank you. Would you like a piece of cake?

B No, thanks. I'm not hungry.

A Would you like something to drink?

B I'd love some water.

A OK. I'll get you some.

B Wait. I brought you a little present.

A Oh, thank you! . . . Oh, Sue! My favorite perfume! Thank you!

B You're welcome. It's from our family.

A That's so nice. Please take some balloons home for your children.

B Thanks. They love balloons.

Lesson D: Reading

Page 128, Exercise 2 – Track 34

Celia had a graduation party last Friday. Her husband sent invitations to Celia's teacher and to their relatives and friends. They all came to the party! Some guests brought gifts for Celia. Her teacher Mrs. Campbell gave her a card. Her Aunt Ana brought her flowers. Her friend Sue gave her some perfume. Her classmate Ruth brought her some cookies. After the party, Celia wrote them thank-you notes. Tomorrow, she is going to mail the thank-you notes at the post office.

Page 129, Exercise 4A – Track 35

1. Thanksgiving
2. Independence Day
3. a wedding
4. a housewarming
5. New Year's Eve
6. Mother's Day
7. Halloween
8. a baby shower
9. Valentine's Day

Illustration credits

Ken Batelman: 86, 87, 88, 119

Travis Foster: 46, 47 *(bottom)*, 107

Chuck Gonzales: 9, 29, 48, 49, 52, 81, 124

Brad Hamann: 11, 21, 35, 89, 114

Ben Kirchner: 2, 4, 6, 7, 12, 18, 19, 24, 32, 33, 38, 44, 45, 50, 58, 59, 64, 70, 71, 76, 84, 85, 90, 96, 97, 102, 110, 111, 116, 122, 123, 128

Jim Kopp: 13, 25, 39, 51, 65, 77, 91, 103, 117, 129

Monika Roe: 17, 36, 37, 62, 75, 115, 127

Lucy Truman: 47 *(top)*, 72, 101

Photography credits

14 ©Punchstock

23 *(clockwise from top left)* ©Jupiter Images; ©Alamy; ©Punchstock; ©Don Mason/Corbis; ©Jupiter Images; ©Livia Corona/Getty Images

29 *(clockwise from top left)* ©Photos.com; ©Alamy; ©Alamy; ©Alamy; ©Michael Kelley/Getty Images; ©Photos.com

34 ©Jupiter Images

42 ©Punchstock

55 ©Larry Williams/Corbis

63 *(top to bottom)* ©Punchstock; ©Getty Images

66 *(top to bottom)* ©Istock Photos; ©Jupiter Images

73 *(top to bottom)* ©Jupiter Images; ©Alamy

74 ©Jupiter Images

78 ©Michael Cogliantry/Getty Images

87 *(left to right)* ©Punchstock; ©Hemera; ©Photos.com; ©Istock Photos

88 *(left to right)* ©Istock Photos; ©Alamy; ©Punchstock; *(inset)* ©Shutterstock

93 ©Shutterstock

98 ©Age Fotostock

121 *(top to bottom)* ©Age Fotostock; ©Jupiter Images; ©Photo Library; ©Billy Hustace/Getty Images; ©Alamy

125 *(clockwise from top left)* ©Alamy; ©Alamy; ©Alamy; ©Istock Photos; ©Age Fotostock; ©Jupiter Images; ©Jupiter Images; ©Alamy; ©Stock Xpert

133 ©Istock Photos